CIVIL WAR TRAIL

ROAD TRIPS

D0095692

This edition written and researched by

**Amy C Balfour, Michael Grosberg, Adam Karlin,
Kevin Raub, Adam Skolnick, Regis St Louis,
and Karla Zimmerman**

HOW TO USE THIS BOOK

Reviews

In the Destinations section:

All reviews are ordered in our authors' preference, starting with their most preferred option. Additionally:

Sights are arranged in the geographic order that we suggest you visit them and, within this order, by author preference.

Eating and Sleeping reviews are ordered by price range (budget, midrange, top end) and, within these ranges, by author preference.

Map Legend

Routes

- Trip Route
- Trip Detour
- Linked Trip
- Walk Route
- Tollway
- Freeway
- Primary
- Secondary
- Tertiary
- Lane
- Unsealed Road
- Plaza/Mall
- Steps
-)= = Tunnel
- Pedestrian Overpass
- Walk Track/Path

Boundaries

- International
- State/Province
- Cliff

Population

- ✪ Capital (National)
- ◉ Capital (State/Province)
- ● City/Large Town
- ○ Town/Village

Transport

- ✈ Airport
- Cable Car/Funicular
- Ⓟ Parking
- Train/Railway
- Ⓣ Tram
- Ⓜ Underground Train Station

Trips

- 1 Trip Numbers
- 9 Trip Stop
- Walking tour
- Trip Detour

Highway Route Markers

- 97 US National Hwy
- 5 US Interstate Hwy
- 44 State Hwy

Hydrography

- River/Creek
- Intermittent River
- Swamp/Mangrove
- Canal
- Water
- Dry/Salt/Intermittent Lake
- Glacier

Areas

- Beach
- Cemetery (Christian)
- Cemetery (Other)
- Park
- Forest
- Reservation
- Urban Area
- Sportsground

Symbols In This Book

✅ Top Tips   🍷 Food & Drink

🔗 Link Your Trips   🌳 Outdoors

💬 Tips from Locals   📷 Essential Photo

↪ Trip Detour   🚶 Walking Tour

📖 History & Culture   🍴 Eating

👪 Family   🛏 Sleeping

⊙ Sights   🛏 Sleeping

🏖 Beaches   🍴 Eating

🏃 Activities   🍷 Drinking

🎓 Courses   ☆ Entertainment

👉 Tours   🔒 Shopping

🎉 Festivals & Events   ⓘ Information & Transport

These symbols and abbreviations give vital information for each listing:

- ✆ Telephone number
- ⊙ Opening hours
- Ⓟ Parking
- ⊖ Nonsmoking
- ❄ Air-conditioning
- @ Internet access
- 🛜 Wi-fi access
- 🏊 Swimming pool
- 🥗 Vegetarian selection
- 📖 English-language menu
- 👪 Family-friendly

- 🐾 Pet-friendly
- 🚍 Bus
- ⛴ Ferry
- 🚊 Tram
- 🚆 Train
- apt apartments
- d double rooms
- dm dorm beds
- q quad rooms
- r rooms
- s single rooms
- ste suites
- tr triple rooms
- tw twin rooms

CONTENTS

DRIVING IN THE USA 120

Manassas Union soldiers head into battle during a reenactment

WELCOME TO
THE CIVIL WAR TRAIL

The Civil War Trail takes in hundreds of miles of Eastern USA. From big cities to backcountry wilds, these are places that helped forge America's identity in those momentous years from 1861–65. Whether you're a history nut, a warrior or a pacifist, battlefields such as Antietam, Manassas, Shiloh or Vicksburg have the power to silence even the busiest mind.

These road trips take you through Virginian backwoods and the nation's capital to the mighty Mississippi and the gracious plantations of the South. And to take in all this region's variety, the physical and cultural landscape behind those peculiar accents and the local delicacies, you have to get in your car and drive.

Follow the routes of the Civil War armies, explore Colonial-era America, sample diverse cuisine, and make pilgrimages to architectural and musical icons – the road awaits.

CIVIL WAR TRAIL

★

3 **Memphis to Nashville**
From juke joints to honky-tonks, music reigns supreme. **3 DAYS**

4 **Historical Mississippi**
A complex history is on display from Oxford to Vicksburg to Natchez. **3 DAYS**

INDIANA

Lima

Lafayette
Danville

Indianapolis
Richmond
Dayton

Terre
Haute
Columbus
Cincinnati

Bloomington

Hoosier
National
Forest
Purchase Unit

Vincennes

Maysville

Frankfort
Lexington

Louisville

Evansville
Henderson
Owensboro
Bardstown
Danville
Berea

Mammoth
Cave
National Park
KENTUCKY
London

Paducah
Bowling
Green
Somerset
Beaver
Creek
Wilderness

Hopkinsville

Paris
Cookeville
Oak
Ridge

ARKANSAS
TENNESSEE
Nashville
Murfreesboro
Knoxville

Jonesboro
Jackson
Columbia
Manchester

Morrilton
Forrest
City
Memphis
Lawrenceburg
Lynchburg
Fayetteville
Cleveland
Chattanooga

Little
Rock
Holly
Springs
Corinth
Florence
Huntsville
Chickamauga and
Chattanooga National
Military Park

Malvern
Pine
Bluff
Stuttgart
Batesville
Clarksdale
Oxford
Decatur
Calhoun

Dumas
Tupelo
Hamilton
Cullman
Rome

Camden
Leland
Winona
West
Point
Jasper
Gadsden
Marietta

El Dorado
Crossett
Starkville
Birmingham
Atlanta

LOUISIANA
Yazoo
City
MISSISSIPPI
Tuscaloosa
Cheaha
Mountain
La Grange

Ruston
Monroe
Vicksburg
Forest
Clanton
Opelika
Columbus

Winnfield
Jackson
Demopolis
Montgomery

Kisatchie
National
Forest
Natchez
Brookhaven
Meridian
Selma
ALABAMA

Mccomb
Laurel
Waynesboro
Greenville
Albany

Baton
Rouge
Hammond
Hattiesburg
Opp
Dothan
Camilla

Opelousas
Gulfport
Mobile
Pensacola
DeFuniak
Springs
Bainbridge
Marianna

Lafayette
Slidell
New
Orleans
Raceland
Pascagoula
Tallahassee
Lynn
Haven
FLORIDA

The Civil War Tour
Preserved battlefields, 19th-century countryside and Southern small towns. **3 DAYS**

Lowcountry & Southern Coast Tour plantations, absorb the culture and try the shrimp and grits. **3 DAYS**

CIVIL WAR
TRAIL
HIGHLIGHTS
★

Antebellum Architecture
Most of the Old South's mansions were torched in the war, which is why the examples in Charleston and Natchez are so compelling. See them on Trips **2** **4**

Music in Memphis & Nashville
Think soul music museums, Beale St clubs, the Country Music Hall of Fame (above) and hell-raising honky-tonks. Hear it all on Trip **3**

Civil War Battlefields
The legacy of this conflict is imprinted on the landscape, especially in places such as Antietam, Manassas and Vicksburg. In summer, many sites host reenactments. See them on Trips **1** **2** **3** **4**

CITY GUIDE

Washington Capitol (p59)

WASHINGTON, DC

The nation's capital is best known to tourists for its superlative monuments and museums, but there's so much more to DC. A staggering amount of the young, ambitious and talented are drawn here, and a burgeoning food, arts and nightlife scene grows every day to accommodate this demographic.

Getting Around

The DC metro (subway) system is the easiest way around town. Five lines – green, red, yellow, orange and blue – connect across town, and fares are based on the distance traveled between stations. The metro is open until midnight Sunday through Thursday and 3am on Friday and Saturday nights.

Parking

Garages are expensive and street parking is a hassle. Numerous restrictions mean it's hard to park longer than two hours anywhere, and many streets are too crowded with cars for parking anyway. Some hotels provide parking for a fee.

Where to Eat

There are great restaurants, generally midrange to high-end (DC has few budget eateries) within easy walking distance of the following metro stops: Gallery Place-Chinatown; U-Street/African-Amer Civil War Memorial/Cardozo; Columbia Heights; Eastern Market; Capitol South; Dupont Circle; Woodley Park-Zoo and Cleveland Park. Georgetown is also a good bet.

Where to Stay

Hotels are sprinkled across town, especially near the following metro stops: Metro Center, Farragut West, Georgetown, Gallery Place-Chinatown, Dupont Circle and Capitol South, as well as Georgetown, off the metro. Try Arlington and Alexandria for cheaper chain-hotel options.

Useful Websites

Washington Metropolitan Area Transit Authority (www.wmata.com)

Washington Post Going Out Guide (www.washingtonpost.com/gog) Events, dining and entertainment.

The Washingtonian (www.washingtonian.com) Covers all elements of DC's cultural scene.

Road Trip through Washington, DC: 1

Destination coverage: p52

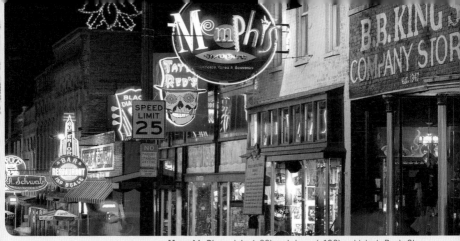

Memphis Blues clubs (p99) and shops (p100) on historic Beale St

MEMPHIS

Memphis is alive with blues, soul and rock and roll, pulsating out of bars, concert halls and...museums? It's a gritty city of warm smiles, smoky barbecue and deep history,

Getting Around

Memphis' best sights are huddled close and demand a stroll. MATA's vintage trolleys ($1, every 12 minutes) ply Main and Front Sts Downtown. Amtrak's **Central Station** (www.amtrak.com; 545 S Main St) is right downtown.

Parking

Metered street parking is available. Parking garages are also abundant, especially around the major sights.

Where to Eat

Locals come to blows over which of the city's chopped-pork sandwiches or dry-rubbed ribs are the best. Barbecue joints are scattered across the city; the ugliest exteriors often yield the tastiest goods. Hip young locals head to the South Main Arts District or Midtown's Cooper-Young or Overton Square neighborhoods, all fashionable evening enclaves.

Where to Stay

Downtown offers plenty of accommodations options. Chain motels lie off I-40, exit 279, across the river in West Memphis, AR. South of Downtown you'll find a number of Elvis-themed places. Look out for the new Guest House at Graceland, a 450-room luxury hotel steps from Graceland.

Useful Websites

Commercial Appeal (www.commercialappeal.com) Daily newspaper with local entertainment listings.

Memphis Flyer (www.memphisflyer.com) Entertainment listings.

Memphis Visitor's Center (www.memphistravel.com) City information center near exit for Graceland.

Tennessee State Visitor Center (www.tnvacation.com) Information on the whole state.

Road Trip through Memphis: 3

Destination coverage: p92

NEED <u>TO</u> KNOW

CELL PHONES
The only foreign phones that work in the USA are GSM tri- or quad-band models. Buy pay-as-you-go cell phones from electronics stores or rent them at major airports.

INTERNET ACCESS
Wi-fi is available at most accommodations and coffee shops. Average rates at city cybercafes are $6 to $12 per hour. Internet access at public libraries is usually free.

FUEL
Gas stations are everywhere, except in some remote areas and national parks. Expect to pay $3.15 to $4.25 per gallon.

RENTAL CARS
Alamo (www.alamo.com)

Car Rental Express (www.carrentalexpress.com)

Enterprise (www.enterprise.com)

Rent-a-Wreck (www.rentawreck.com)

IMPORTANT NUMBERS
AAA (☎800-222-4357) Roadside assistance for auto-club members.

Emergency (☎911)

Directory Assistance (☎411)

Operator (☎0)

Climate

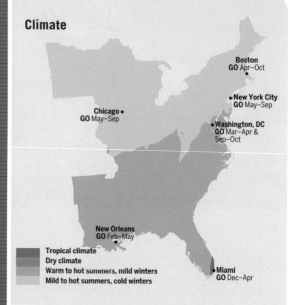

Boston
GO Apr–Oct

New York City
GO May–Sep

Chicago
GO May–Sep

Washington, DC
GO Mar–Apr & Sep–Oct

New Orleans
GO Feb–May

Miami
GO Dec–Apr

Tropical climate
Dry climate
Warm to hot summers, mild winters
Mild to hot summers, cold winters

When to Go

High Season (Jun–Aug)
» Spring and summer music festivals sprout in Tennessee and Mississippi.

» Warm days nationwide, with generally high temperatures.

» Rooms can be scarce and should be booked well ahead.

Shoulder Season (Apr–May & Sep–Oct)
» Milder temperatures; hurricane season peaks (Aug–Nov) on the Atlantic coast.

» Spring wildflowers (Apr–May) and autumn foliage (Sep–Oct) in many areas.

» Room prices drop from their peak by 20% to 30%.

Low Season (Nov–Mar)
» Colder wintry days, with snowfall and heavy rainstorms in many regions.

» Lowest prices on lodgings, except at ski resorts and warm, sunny destinations.

» Many attractions open fewer days and shorter hours.

Daily Costs

Budget: Less than $100
» Hostel dorm bed: $25–40; campsite: $10–40; cheap motel room: $50–100

» Roadside diner or take-out meal: $10–15

» Hit the beach, find a park and keep an eye out for discount days at museums

Midrange: $100–200
» Two-star hotel room: $100–200

» Casual sit-down restaurant meal: $25–40

» Rental car: from $30 per day, excluding insurance and gas

» State and national park entry: $5–25 (some free)

Top End: Over $200
» Resort hotel room: from $250

» Three-course meal in top restaurant: $75–100

Eating

Diners, drive-ins & cafes Cheap, simple and occasionally with homemade food.

Seafood shacks Casual waterfront kitchens.

Brewpubs & gastropubs Regional craft beers and wines, 'pub grub' from hearty to high-end cuisine.

Vegetarians & other diets Can often be catered for, especially in cities.

Eating price indicators represent the cost of a main course:

$	less than $10
$$	$10–20
$$$	more than $20

Sleeping

Camping Ranging from amenity-rich RV parks to primitive wilderness sites.

Motels Everywhere along highways, around cities and in heavily touristed spots.

Hotels & hostels Common in metro areas and popular tourist destinations.

B&Bs Smaller, often historic and romantic, but pricey.

Sleeping price indicators represent the cost of a room with private bath, excluding taxes:

$	less than $100
$$	$100–200
$$$	more than $200

Arriving in the USA

Major US airports offer free inter-terminal transportation and car-rental shuttles.

Los Angeles International Airport (LAX)

Taxis $30–55; 30 to 60 minutes.

Door-to-door shuttles Around $16–$25.

Public transportation Shuttle C (free) to LAX City Bus Center or Shuttle G (free) to Metrorail's Aviation Station; LAX FlyAway Bus to downtown Union Station ($7; 30 to 50 minutes).

John F Kennedy International Airport (JFK, New York)

Taxis $45–65; 35 to 90 minutes.

Door-to-door shuttles Around $16–24.

Public transportation AirTrain ($5) to Jamaica Station for MTA subway and bus connections ($2.50; 50 to 75 minutes) or LIRR trains ($10.50; 35 minutes) into Manhattan.

Money

ATMs are practically everywhere. Credit cards are almost universally accepted and often required for making reservations (debit cards are sometimes OK).

Tipping

Tipping is expected, not optional: 15% to 20% at restaurants, 10% to 15% for bartenders and taxi drivers, and $2 per bag for porters.

Opening Hours

Opening hours may be shorter in winter (November to March).

Restaurants ⏱7–10:30am, 11:30am–2:30pm and 5–9pm daily, some later Friday and Saturday

Shops ⏱10am–6pm Monday to Saturday, noon–5pm Sunday (malls close later)

Useful Websites

Lonely Planet (www.lonely planet.com/usa) Destination information, hotel and hostel bookings, traveler forums and more.

Civil War Trails (www.civil wartrails.org) Detailed resource for Civil War Trail tourists.

Roadside America (www. roadsideamerica.com) For everything weird and wacky.

For more information, see Driving in the USA (p120)

Road Trips

1 The Civil War Tour, 3 Days
See preserved battlefields, 19th-century countryside, museums aplenty and Southern small towns. (p17)

2 Lowcountry & Southern Coast, 3 Days
Visit the spot where the first shots of the Civil War were fired, along with antebellum architecture and coastal scenery. (p27)

3 Memphis to Nashville, 3 Days
Classic Blues and Bluegrass are your soundtrack to whiskey stops and important battlefield sites. (p35)

4 Historical Mississippi, 3 Days
Mississippi's complex history is on display, from the Civil War to civil rights. (p43)

Mississippi Historic township along Natchez Trace Parkway (p48)
UNIVERSALIMAGESGROUP/CONTRIBUTOR/LONELY PLANET/GETTY IMAGES ©

The Civil War Tour

Virginia and Maryland pack many of the seminal sites of America's bloodiest war into a space that includes some of the Eastern seaboard's most attractive countryside.

TRIP HIGHLIGHTS

START Antietam
Frederick

105 miles

Manassas National Battlefield Park
Wander Bull Run's bucolic fields

 WASHINGTON, DC

153 miles

Fredericksburg
Deep-forest parks hide this battlefield

230 miles

Richmond
Enjoy historic hotels, great eats and magnificent museums

FINISH

Petersburg

320 miles

Appomattox Court House National Park
Where the war, and your trip, ends

**3 DAYS
320 MILES / 515KM**

GREAT FOR...

BEST TIME TO GO
September to November for sunny skies and autumnal color shows at preserved battlefields.

ESSENTIAL PHOTO
The fences and fields of Antietam at sunset.

BEST FOR FOODIES
Lamb burgers at Richmond's Burger Bach (p76).

Fredericksburg Locals reenact Civil War battles (p20)

17

MICHAEL MELFORD/GETTY IMAGES ©

1 The Civil War Tour

The Civil War was fought from 1861–65 in the nation's backyards, and many of those backyards are between Washington, DC, and Richmond. On this trip you will cross battlefields where over 100,000 Americans perished and are buried, foe next to foe. Amid rolling farmlands, sunny hills and deep forests, you'll discover a jarring juxtaposition of bloody legacy and bucolic scenery, and, along the way, the places where America forged its identity.

1 Antietam (p71)

While most of this trip takes place in Virginia, there is Civil War ground to be covered in neighboring Maryland, a border state officially allied with the Union yet close enough to the South to have Southern sympathies. Confederate General Robert E Lee, hoping to capitalize on a friendly populace, tried to invade Maryland early in the conflict. The subsequent Battle of Antietam, fought in Sharpsburg, MD, on September 17, 1862, has the dubious distinction of marking the bloodiest day in American history. The battle site is preserved at **Antietam National Battlefield** (☎ 301-432-5124; www.nps.gov/anti; 5831 Dunker Church Rd, Sharpsburg; ⊕ 9am-5pm) in the corn-and-hill country of north-central Maryland.

As befits an engagement that claimed 23,000 casualties in the course of a single, nightmarish day, even the local geographic nomenclature has become violent. An area previously known as the Sunken Road turned into 'Bloody

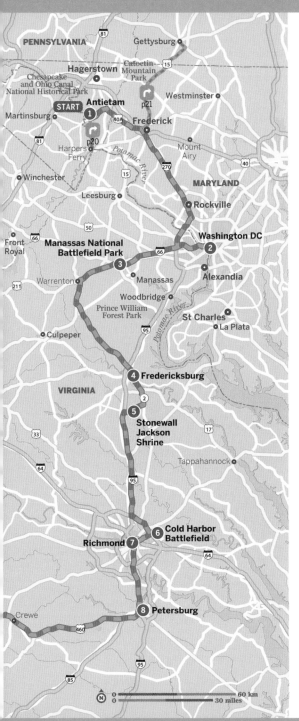

Lane' after bodies were stacked there. In the park's cemetery, many of the Union gravestones bear the names of Irish and German immigrants who died in a country they had only recently adopted.

The Drive » Take MD-65 south out of Antietam to the town of Sharpsburg. From here, take MD-34 east for 6 miles, then turn right onto US 40A (eastbound). Take US 40A for 11 miles, then merge onto US 70 south, followed 3 miles later by US 270 (bypassing Frederick). Take 270 south to the Beltway (I-495); access exit 45B to get to I-66 east, which will eventually lead you to the National Mall, where the next stops are located.

❷ Washington, DC (p52)

Washington, DC, was the capital of the Union during the Civil War, just as it is the capital of the country today. While the city was never invaded by the Confederacy, thousands of Union soldiers passed through, trained and drilled inside of the city; indeed, the official name of the North's main fighting force was the Army of the Potomac.

The **National Museum of American History** (www.americanhistory.si.edu; cnr 14th St & Constitution Ave NW; ☺10am-5:30pm; 🚻), located on the National Mall, has good exhibitions on the Civil War. Perhaps more importantly, it provides visitors with the context for understanding why the war happened.

19

Following the war, a grateful nation erected many monuments to Union generals. One worth visiting is the **African American Civil War Memorial** (www.afroamcivilwar.org; cnr U St & Vermont Ave NW), inscribed with the names of soldiers of color who served in the Union army.

The Drive » From Washington, DC, it takes about an hour along I-66W to reach Manassas.

TRIP HIGHLIGHT

❸ Manassas National Battlefield Park (Bull Run; p72)

The site of the first major pitched battle of the Civil War is mere minutes from the strip malls of Northern Virginia. NPS-run **Manassas National Battlefield Park** (📞703-361-1339; www.nps.gov/mana; 12521 Lee Hwy; adult/child $3/free, film $3; ⊙8:30am-5pm, tours 11:15am, 12:15pm, 2:15pm Jun-Aug) occupies the site where, in 1861, 35,000 Union soldiers and 32,500 Confederates saw the view you have today: a stretch of gorgeous countryside that has miraculously survived the predations of the Army of Northern Virginia real-estate developers.

This is as close as many will come to 19th-century rural America; distant hills, dark, brooding tree lines, low curving fields and the soft hump of overgrown trench works.

Following the battle, both sides realized a long war was at hand. Europe watched nervously; in a matter of weeks, the largest army in the world was the Union Army of the Potomac. The second biggest was the Confederate States of America Army. A year later, at the Battle of Shiloh, 24,000 men listed as casualties – more than all the accumulated casualties of every previous American war combined.

The Drive » In Manassas, take US 29N for 13 miles and then turn left onto US 17S (Marsh Rd). Follow it south for about 35 miles to get to downtown Fredericksburg.

TRIP HIGHLIGHT

❹ Fredericksburg (p72)

If battlefields preserve rural America, Fredericksburg is an example of what the nation's main streets once looked like: orderly grids, touches of green and friendly storefronts. But for all its cuteness, this is the site of one of the worst blunders in American military history. In 1862, when the Northern Army attempted a massed charge against an entrenched Confederate position, a Southern artilleryman looked at the bare slope that Union forces had to cross and told a commanding officer,

DETOUR: JOHN BROWN WAX MUSEUM, HARPERS FERRY

Start: ❶ Antietam

For those who appreciate kitsch and history, the ultimate attraction to seek out in these parts is the **John Brown Wax Museum** (📞304-535-6342; www.johnbrownwaxmuseum.com; 168 High St, Harpers Ferry; adult/child $7/5; ⊙9am-4:30pm, 10am-5:30pm summer).

A white abolitionist, Brown led an ill-conceived slave rebellion in Harpers Ferry that helped spark the Civil War. Brown was described as eccentric at best, and perhaps mad at worst, by contemporaries, but Frederick Douglass – a leader of the abolitionist movement – held him up as a hero, and wrote: 'Had some other men made such a display of rigid virtue, I should have rejected it, as affected, false, or hypocritical, but in John Brown, I felt it to be as real as iron or granite.'

Stirring stuff, right? It is, which is why there's a cognitive disconnect when you visit the wax museum dedicated to Brown's life. The spot is old-school, but well worth a visit for all that.

DETOUR:
GETTYSBURG NATIONAL MILITARY PARK

Start: ❶ Antietam

The Battle of Gettysburg, fought in Gettysburg, PA, in July of 1863, marked the turning point of the war and the high-water mark of the Confederacy's attempted rebellion. Lee never made a gambit as bold as this invasion of the North, and his army (arguably) never recovered from the defeat it suffered here.

Gettysburg National Military Park (☏717-334-1124; www.nps.gov/gett; 1195 Baltimore Pike; adult/child $12.50/8.50, incl museum & visitor center; ⊘park 6am-10pm Apr-Oct, to 7pm Nov-Mar, museum 8am-6pm Apr-Oct, to 5pm Nov-Mar) does an excellent job of explaining the course and context of the combat. Look for Little Round Top Hill, where a Union unit checked a Southern flanking maneuver, and the field of Pickett's Charge, where the Confederacy suffered its most crushing defeat up to that point. Following the battle Abraham Lincoln gave his Gettysburg Address here to mark the victory and the 'new birth of the nation' on said country's birthday: July 4.

You can easily lose a day here just soaking up the scenery – a gorgeous swath of rolling hills and lush forest interspersed with hollows, rock formations and farmland. To get here, jump on US 15 northbound in Frederick, MD, during the drive between Antietam and Washington, DC. Follow 15 north for 35 miles to Gettysburg.

'A chicken could not live on that field when we open on it.' Sixteen charges resulted in an estimated 6000 to 8000 Union casualties.

Fredericksburg & Spotsylvania National Military Park (www.nps.gov/frsp) is not as immediately compelling as Manassas because of the thick forest that still covers the battlefields, but the woods themselves are a sylvan wonder. Again, the pretty nature of...well, nature, grows over graves; the nearby Battle of the Wilderness was named for these thick woods, which caught fire, killing hundreds of wounded soldiers after the shooting was finished.

The Drive » From Fredericksburg, take US 17 south for 5 miles, after which 17 becomes VA-2 (also known as Sandy Lane Dr and Fredericksburg Turnpike). Follow this road for 5 more miles, then turn right onto Stonewall Jackson Rd (State Rd 606).

---

❺ Stonewall Jackson Shrine

In Chancellorsville, Robert E Lee, outnumbered two to one, split his forces and attacked both flanks of the Union army. The audacity of the move caused the Northern force to crumble and flee across the Potomac River, but the victory was costly; in the course of the fighting, Lee's ablest general, Stonewall

Jackson, had his arm shot off by a nervous Confederate sentry (the arm is buried near the Fredericksburg National Park visitor center; ask a ranger for directions there).

The wound was patched, but Jackson went on to contract a fatal dose of pneumonia. He was taken to what is now the next stop on this tour: the **Stonewall Jackson Shrine** (☏804-633-6076; 12019 Stonewall Jackson Rd, Woodford; ⊘9am-5pm) in nearby Guinea Station. In a small white cabin set against attractive Virginia horse-country, overrun with sprays of purple flowers and daisy fields, Jackson uttered a series of prolonged ramblings. Then he fell

WHY THIS IS A CLASSIC TRIP
ADAM KARLIN, AUTHOR

Want to see some of the finest countryside left in the Eastern seaboard, while simultaneously exploring the contradictions, struggles and triumphs at the root of the American experiment? Yeah, we thought so. The Civil War Tour allows travelers to access the formative spaces of the nation, all set against a backdrop of lush fields, dark forests, dirt-rutted country lanes and the immense weight of history.

Top: Stonewall Jackson Shrine (p21)
Left: Manassas National Battlefield Park (p20)
Right: Monument on Bloody Lane, Antietam National Battlefield (p18)

silent, whispered, 'Let us cross over the river and rest in the shade of the trees,' and died.

The Drive » You can get here via I-95, which you take to I-295S (then take exit 34A), which takes 50 minutes. Or, for a back road experience (one hour, 10 minutes), take VA-2S south for 35 miles until it connects to VA-643/Rural Point Rd. Stay on VA-643 until it becomes VA-156/Cold Harbor Rd, which leads to the battlefield.

⑥ Cold Harbor Battlefield

By 1864 Union General Ulysses S Grant was ready to take the battle into Virginia. His subsequent invasion, dubbed the Overland (or Wilderness) Campaign, was one of the bloodiest of the war. It reached a violent climax at Cold Harbor, just north of Richmond.

At the site now known as **Cold Harbor Battlefield** (☎804-226-1981; www.nps.gov/rich; 5515 Anderson-Wright Dr, Mechanicsville, VA; ☼sunrise-sunset, visitor center 9am-4:30pm), Grant threw his men into a full frontal assault; the resultant casualties were horrendous, and a precursor to WWI trench warfare.

The area has reverted to a forest and field checkerboard overseen by the National Park Service. Ask a ranger to direct you to the third turnout, a series of Union earthworks from where you can look out at the most preserved section of the battlefield: the long, low field Northern soldiers charged across. This landscape has essentially not changed in over 150 years.

The Drive » From Cold Harbor, head north on VA-156/Cold Harbor Rd for about 3 miles until it intersects Creighton Rd. Turn left on Creighton and follow it for 6 miles into Richmond.

TRIP HIGHLIGHT

❼ Richmond (p73)

There are two Civil War museums in the former capital of the Confederacy, and they make for an interesting study in contrasts. The **Museum of the Confederacy** (MOC; ☏804-649-1861; www.moc.org; 1201 E Clay St; adult/child $10/8; ⊘10am-5pm)

was once a shrine to the Southern 'Lost Cause,' and still attracts a fair degree of neo-Confederate types. But the MOC has graduated into a respected educational institution, and its collection of Confederate artifacts is probably the best in the country. The optional tour of the Confederate White House is recommended for its quirky insights (did you know the second-most powerful man in the Confederacy may have been a gay Jew?).

On the other hand, the **American Civil War Center** (☏804-780-1865; www.tredegar.org; 490 Tredegar St; adult/child $10/8; ⊘9am-5pm; ♿), located in the old Tredegar ironworks (the main armament producer for the Confederacy), presents the war from three

perspectives: Northern, Southern and African American. Exhibits are well presented and insightful. The effect is clearly powerful and occasionally divisive, a testament to the conflict's lasting impact.

The Drive » Take Rte 95 southbound for about 23 miles and get on exit 52. Get onto 301 (Wythe St) and follow until it becomes Washington St, and eventually VA-35/Oaklawn Dr. Look for signs to the battlefield park from here.

❽ Petersburg (p77)

Petersburg, just south of Richmond, is the blue-collar sibling city to the Virginia capital, its center gutted by white flight following desegregation. **Petersburg National Battlefield Park** (nps.gov/pete; US 36; vehicle/pedestrian $5/3; ⊘9am-5pm) marks the spot where Northern and Southern soldiers spent almost a quarter of the war in a protracted, trench-induced standoff.

The Battle of the Crater, made well-known in Charles Frazier's *Cold Mountain*, was an attempt by Union soldiers to break this stalemate by tunneling under the Confederate lines and blowing up their fortifications; the end result was Union soldiers caught in the hole wrought by their own sabotage, killed like fish in a barrel.

WHAT'S IN A NAME?

Although the Civil War is the widely accepted label for the conflict covered in this trip, you'll still hear die-hard Southern boosters refer to the period as the 'War Between the States.' What's the difference? Well, a Civil War implies an armed insurrection against a ruling power that never lost its privilege to govern, whereas the name 'War Between the States' suggests said states always had (and still have) a right to secession from the Republic.

Another naming convention of the war goes thus: while the North preferred to name battles for defining geographic terms (Bull Run, Antietam), Southern officers named them for nearby towns (Manassas, Sharpsburg). Although most Americans refer to battles by their Northern names, in some areas folks simply know Manassas as the Battle Of, not as the strip mall with a good Waffle House.

The Drive » Drive south of Petersburg, then west through back roads to follow Lee's last retreat. There's an excellent map available at www.civilwartraveler.com; we prefer taking VA-460 west from Petersburg, then connecting to VA-635, which leads to Appomattox via VA-24, near Farmville.

TRIP HIGHLIGHT

⑨ Appomattox Court House National Park (p78)

About 92 miles west of Petersburg is **Appomattox Court House National Park** (☎434-352-8987; www.nps.gov/apco; vehicle $10; ⏱8:30am-5pm), where the Confederacy finally surrendered. The park is wide and lovely, and the staff are helpful.

There are several marker stones dedicated to the surrendering Confederates; the most touching one marks the spot where Robert E Lee rode back from Appomattox after surrendering to Union General Ulysses S Grant. Lee's soldiers stood on either side of the field waiting for the return of their commander. When Lee rode into sight he doffed his hat; the troops surged toward him, some saying goodbye while others, too overcome to speak, passed their hands over the flanks of Lee's horse. The spot's dedicated to defeat, humility and reconciliation, and the imperfect realization of all those qualities is the character of the America you've been driving through.

Lowcountry & Southern Coast

2

Century-old churches, timeless marshes, ancient oaks and Spanish moss: on this Lowcountry loop, the past rises up to say hello. Except on Parris Island, where it yells, 'Move it marine!'

TRIP HIGHLIGHTS

20 miles

Middleton Place
Meditate in beauty in sprawling gardens designed in 1741

15 miles

Drayton Hall
This 1738 plantation survived two wars

3 **2** **START/ FINISH** ● Charleston

Jacksonboro

Yemassee

Edisto Beach

128 miles

Hunting Island State Park
Watch the sun set over the marsh

6 **7** **8**

Marine Corps Recruit Depot
Learn about Navajo Code Talkers in the museum

119 miles

Penn Center
Martin Luther King strategized here in the 1960s

105 miles

3 DAYS
265 MILES / 426KM

GREAT FOR...

BEST TIME TO GO

From spring to fall for the Gullah Festival, produce at roadside stands and sunshine for outdoor fun.

 ESSENTIAL PHOTO

Sunset at Hunting Island State Park.

 BEST FOR CULTURE

Learning the traditions of unique coastal communities, from boot camp to bottle trees.

Beaufort Antebellum architecture abounds in this charming town (p30)

Lowcountry & Southern Coast

The Lowcountry welcomes travelers with a warm embrace – straight from the 1700s. This coastal region, which stretches from Charleston south to Georgia, is a tangle of islands, inlets and tidal marshes. This drive sweeps in plantation life, military history, Gullah culture and a landmark African American school, all set against a moody backdrop of coastal wilds.

① Charleston (p82)

Charleston is a city for savoring. Stroll past Rainbow Row, take a carriage ride, study the antebellum architecture and enjoy shrimp and grits. Historically, the city is best known for its role in the start of the Civil War. The first shots of the conflict rang out on April 12, 1861, at **Fort Sumter**, a pentagon-shaped island in the harbor. **Boat tours** (☑ boat tour 843-722-2628, park 843-883-3123; www.nps.gov/fosu; 340 Concord St;

adult/child $19/12; ☺ tours 9:30am, noon & 2:30pm summer, fewer winter) depart from Aquarium Wharf at the eastern end of Calhoun St, and from Patriot's Point in Mt Pleasant.

The Drive >> From the wharf, follow Calhoun St west through Charleston to Hwy 61, also known as Ashley River Rd. Follow it north for about 10 miles.

TRIP HIGHLIGHT

② Drayton Hall

Three plantations – Drayton Hall, Magnolia Plantation and Middleton Place – border Ashley River Rd, their gardens, swamps and graveyards hidden behind a line of oaks and Spanish moss.

The first plantation on the drive is **Drayton Hall** (☑ 843-769-2600; www.draytonhall.org; 3380 Ashley River Rd; adult/child $22/10; ☺ 9am-5pm Mon-Sat, 11am-5pm Sun, last tour

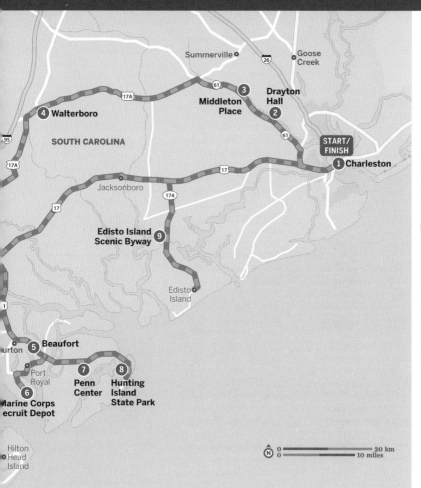

3:30pm), built in 1738 and unique for its Georgian-Palladian architecture. It was the only plantation along the Ashley River to survive the Revolutionary and Civil Wars. It also survived the great earthquake of 1886. The plantation is unique because it has been preserved, but not restored. After a guided tour of the house, stroll the grounds on paths wandering along the river and around a marsh.

The Drive » Continue north on Ashley River Rd/Hwy 61. Pass Magnolia Plantation then drive another 3 miles. After passing the exit to Middleton Inn, turn right for the gardens.

TRIP HIGHLIGHT

3 Middleton Place

Designed in 1741, the vast gardens at **Middleton Place** (☏843-556-6020; www.middletonplace.org; 4300 Ashley River Rd; gardens adult/child $28/10, house tours add $15; ⊙9am-5pm) are the oldest in the US. One hundred slaves spent a decade terracing and digging the precise geometric canals. The property was the Middleton family seat from the 1700s through the Civil War.

The grounds are a mix of classic formal French gardens and romantic woodland settings – one lonely path leads to a band of stone cherubs blissfully rocking out. There are also flooded rice paddies and fields of rare-breed farm animals. Union soldiers burned the main house in 1855, but a guest wing, built in 1755 and later restored, still stands today. It contains a museum with Middleton family furnishings and historical documents.

Enjoy she-crab soup and other Lowcountry dishes at the highly regarded **Middleton Place Restaurant** (☎843-266-7477; www.middletonplace.org; 4300 Ashley River Rd; lunch $13-16, dinner $14-34; ⊙noon-3pm & 6-8pm Tue-Thu & Sun, 6-9pm Fri & Sat).

The Drive ≫ Follow Hwy 61 north to its junction with US 17A. Turn left. Take US 17A south for 24 miles.

─ ─ ─ ─ ─ ─ ─ ─ ─ ─

④ **Walterboro**

The town of Walterboro calls itself the 'The Front Porch of the Lowcountry,' and a red rocking chair greets guests at the **welcome center** (☎843-538-4353; 1273 Sniders Hwy; ⊙9am-5pm Mon-Sat). Downtown, shoppers can peruse a dozen antique stores before visiting the **South Carolina Artisans Center** (www.scartisanscenter.com; 318 Wichman St; ⊙9am-5pm Mon-Sat, 1-5pm Sun). Here, folk art, fine art and traditional crafts fill several rooms in a rambling house.

Boardwalks and trails wind through 842 acres of swampland at the new **Walterboro Wildlife Sanctuary** (www.walterborosc.org). One path tracks the Savannah Stage Coach Rd, which dates to Colonial times. Entrances are off Jefferies Blvd at Beach Rd and Detreville St. The park's

original name, the Great Swamp Sanctuary, was scrapped in 2013 because the town council thought the word 'swamp' had negative connotations, especially for urban visitors. We beg to differ.

The Drive ≫ From Walterboro, continue south on US 17A to Yemassee. For brochures and history, turn right at US 17 and continue to the Low Country Visitor Center at Frampton Plantation. Otherwise, turn left on US 17 and continue to Beaufort.

─ ─ ─ ─ ─ ─ ─ ─ ─ ─

⑤ **Beaufort (p88)**

The streets are lined with antebellum homes. Magnolias drip with Spanish moss. Boats shimmer on the river. Gobs of cafes and galleries crowd downtown. The town is so darn charming that it's often the backdrop for Hollywood films set in the South, from *The Big Chill* and *The Prince of Tides* to *Forrest Gump*. Walk, eat, shop...or just nap on the porch at your B&B.

The Drive ≫ Take the Sea Island Pkwy over the river then turn right onto US 21N, following it about 5½ miles to Parris Island. Take the first exit toward Malecon Dr. Follow the signs to the museum.

─ ─ ─ ─ ─ ─ ─ ─ ─ ─

TRIP HIGHLIGHT

⑥ **Marine Corps Recruit Depot (p88)**

More than 17,000 men and women endure boot

BLUE BOTTLE TREES

That tree in the distance? The one with the branches sprouting empty blue bottles? Say hello to your first bottle tree, a tradition that traces back to 9th-century Congo. According to lore, haunts and evil spirits, being of a curious nature, crawl inside the bottles to see what they can find. They become trapped and then are destroyed by the morning sunlight. Stop and listen. On a windy night you might just hear them moan.

Charleston House and grounds at Middleton Place (p29)

camp each year at the Parris Island recruiting depot (www.mcrdpi.usmc.mil), which has trained marines since 1915. The experience was made notorious by Stanley Kubrick's *Full Metal Jacket*.

The Modern Marine Wing at the **Parris Island Museum** (☎843-228-2951; www.parrisislandmuseum.com; 111 Panama St; admission free; ☺10am-4:30pm) describes marine participation in recent wars. Check out the **Navajo Code Talkers** display – not one of their transmissions was ever compromised during WWII. Another exhibit spotlights famous former marines, including Gene Hackman, Shaggy and George Jones. Check the website for dates for the popular **Friday graduations**. You may be asked to show ID and car registration before driving onto the grounds.

The Drive ❯❯ Return to the Sea Island Pkwy and turn right. Drive almost 5 miles east to Dr Martin Luther King Jr Dr. Turn right.

- - - - - - - - - - - - -

TRIP HIGHLIGHT

❼ Penn Center (p89)

East of Beaufort is a series of marshy, rural islands including St Helena Island, considered the heart of Gullah country. The nonprofit **Penn Center** (☎843-838-2474; www.penncenter.com/museum; 16 Penn Center Circle W; adult/child 6-16yr $5/3; ☺9am-4pm Mon-Sat) preserves and celebrates Sea Island culture. Here, the **York W Bailey Museum** traces the history of Penn School, established in 1862, which was one of the nation's first schools for freed slaves. Martin Luther King used the site in the 1960s as a retreat for strategic, nonviolent planning during the Civil Rights movement.

The Drive ❯❯ Return to the Sea Island Pkwy. Follow it east over expansive marshes then cross the Harbor River Bridge.

- - - - - - - - - - - - -

TRIP HIGHLIGHT

❽ Hunting Island State Park (p89)

With its tidal lagoons, maritime forest, bone-white beach, and 3000 acres of salt marsh, **Hunting Island State Park** (☎843-838-2011; www.southcarolinaparks.com; 2555 Sea Island Pkwy; adult/child $5/3, tent sites $17-38, cabins $210; ☺visitor center 9am-5pm Mon-Fri, 11am-5pm Sat & Sun) is a nature lover's dream. There are also 8 miles of hiking and biking trails. On a rainy day, try climbing the 175 steps inside the **lighthouse** (admission $2; ☺10am-4:45pm Mar-Oct), with lofty views of the coast as your reward. At the **nature center** (⊙9am-5pm Tue-Sat, open daily Jun-Aug) you can learn about local wildlife. The boardwalk behind the nature center is a great place to catch the sunset. The park was also the setting for the Vietnam War scenes in *Forrest Gump*, which were filmed in the marsh.

The Drive » Backtrack north on US 21 to its junction with US 17N. Drive almost 30 miles. Turn right onto Hwy 174.

- - - - - - - - - -

❾ Edisto Island Scenic Byway (p88)

With its old churches, grassy marshes, and moss-draped oaks, the 17-mile Edisto Island Scenic Byway is a classic Lowcountry drive. It stretches along Hwy 174 from the Atlantic Intracoastal Waterway south to Edisto Beach State Park.

Swoop over the waterway then take the first right to the **Dawhoo Landing** parking area. A map here lists byway attractions. Turn around for a nice view of the graceful McKinley Washington, Jr Bridge. Continue south to **King's Farm Market** (p88) for local produce, baked goods, jams and Cheerwine.

For history, visit the sometimes-open **Edisto Island Museum** and the 1831 **Presbyterian Church**. Next up? The snakey **Edisto Island Serpentarium** (www .edistoserpentarium.com; 1374 Hwy 174; adult/child $15/11; ⊙10am-6pm Mon-Sat Jun–mid-Aug, hours vary Thu-Sat spring & fall, closed winter) followed by the mystery tree – look right, into the marsh, to see its seasonal decorations. Last is **Edisto Beach State Park** (☎843-869- 2156; www.southcarolinaparks .com; adult/child $5/3, tent sites from $21, furnished cabins from $110), with camping just steps from the shore. From here, return to Charleston.

Hunting Island State Park Lighthouse (p31)

DANIELA DUNCAN/GETTY IMAGES ©

Memphis to Nashville

3

When two of America's legendary musical towns are within three hours of one another, they must be linked. Your journey will include a shot of history (and whiskey) along the way.

TRIP HIGHLIGHTS

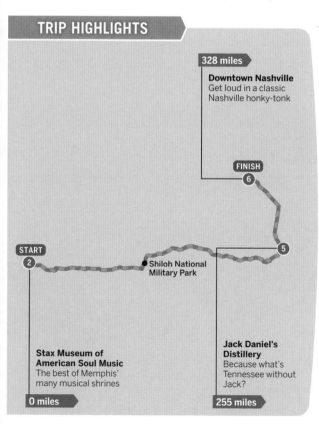

328 miles

Downtown Nashville
Get loud in a classic Nashville honky-tonk

FINISH
6

START
2

● Shiloh National Military Park

5

Stax Museum of American Soul Music
The best of Memphis' many musical shrines

0 miles

Jack Daniel's Distillery
Because what's Tennessee without Jack?

255 miles

---

3 DAYS
328 MILES / 528KM

GREAT FOR...

BEST TIME TO GO
March to June and September to November for welcome weather and tasty music festivals.

ESSENTIAL PHOTO
Sun Studio, ground zero for American rock and roll.

BEST FOR MUSIC
The entire route, from the blues, rock and soul to bluegrass and country.

Stax Museum of American Soul Music Full of the stories of soul legends (p37)

STEPHEN SAKS/GETTY IMAGES ©

3 Memphis to Nashville

Memphis is a warm summer night on the riverside. Nashville is a springtime picnic in the sun. Memphis is a smoky blues club, a twisted history and sweet memories. Nashville is a glamour girl – a fine Southern town with cowboy crass, platinum-blonde diamond beauty and beer-soaked stages. Nashville is bluegrass. Memphis is blues. There's a tug of war between Memphis and Nashville devotees. But why choose sides when you can enjoy their differences?

❶ Beale Street & Around (p93)

By the early 1900s Beale St was the hub of African American social and civic activity, becoming an early center for what was to be known as blues music. In the '50s and '60s, local recording companies cut tracks for blues, soul, R&B and rockabilly artists such as Al Green, Johnny Cash and Elvis, cementing Memphis' place in the American music firmament. Sprinkled on Memphis' most famous block are **BB**

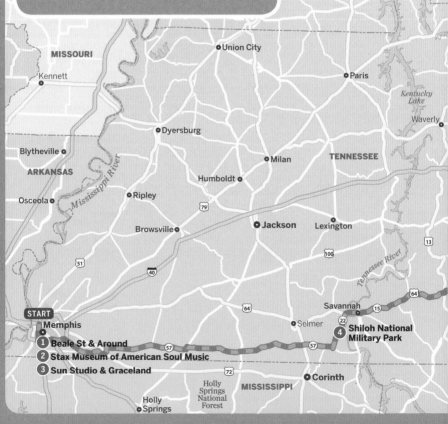

MISSOURI

Kennett

○ Union City

○ Paris

Kentucky Lake

Waverly ○

○ Dyersburg

Blytheville ○

○ Milan

TENNESSEE

ARKANSAS

Mississippi River

Humboldt ○

Osceola ○   ○ Ripley

79

Browsville ○

○ Jackson   Lexington

13

51

100

Tennessee River

40

64

START
Memphis

Savannah

Selmer

64

15

64

22

❹ **Shiloh National Military Park**

❶ **Beale St & Around**

57

57

❷ **Stax Museum of American Soul Music**

❸ **Sun Studio & Graceland**

72

○ Corinth

Holly Springs National Forest

MISSISSIPPI

Holly ○ Springs

King's (☎901-524-5464; www.bbkingclubs.com; 143 Beale St; ☉11am-2am, kitchen open until 11pm), the original nightclub from the Mississippi kid who came to Memphis and became a star; the **New Daisy Theater** (☎901-525-8981; www.newdaisy.com; 330 Beale St), which regularly hosts indie rock acts; and **A Schwab's** (☎901-523-9782; www.a-schwab.com; 163 Beale St; ☉noon-5pm Mon-Thu, 10am-9pm Fri & Sat, 11am-5pm Sun), with three floors of quirk – don't miss the cool antique gallery upstairs.

Gibson Beale Street Showcase (www.gibson. com; 145 Lt George W Lee Ave; admission $10, no children under 5; ☉tours 11am-4pm Mon-Sat, noon-4pm Sun) offers a fascinating 45-minute tour where you can see master craftspeople transform solid blocks of wood into legendary Gibson guitars. Journey back into the roots of American popular music at Memphis Rock 'n' Soul Museum (p93). Its audio tour has over 100 songs, and explains how gospel, country

and blues mingled in the Mississippi Delta to create a modern sound. The blues are palpable once again when you visit the National Civil Rights Museum (p93), which chronicles the ongoing struggles for African American freedom and equality in the US.

The Drive » Make your way over to 3rd St then head south to E McLemore Ave, where the ragged edge of Memphis begins to show.

TRIP HIGHLIGHT

❷ Stax Museum of American Soul Music (p95)

There are few (or no) funkier places on earth than the birthplace of soul music. The **Stax** (☎901-942-7685; www. staxmuseum.com; 926 E McLemore Ave; adult/child $13/10; ☉10am-5pm Tue-Sat, from 1pm Sun) experience begins with a moving 20-minute introductory film and the exhibits build on that. This is the label that used an integrated house band to back legends like Sam Cooke, Booker T Jones, and the amazing Otis Redding. Ike Turner is given reverence as the visionary he was. His guitar and Tina's dress are on display (his domestic violence history conspicuously absent). Named for brother-sister founders Jim Stewart and Estelle Axton, the studio always had a record shop in

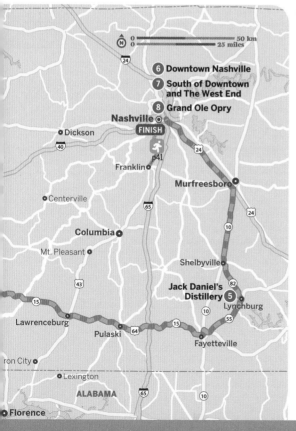

6 Downtown Nashville
7 South of Downtown and The West End
8 Grand Ole Opry
Nashville ◉ FINISH
Dickson
Franklin
Murfreesboro
Centerville
Columbia
Mt. Pleasant
Shelbyville
Jack Daniel's Distillery 5
Lynchburg
Lawrenceburg
Pulaski
Fayetteville
ron City
Lexington
ALABAMA
Florence
0 — 50 km
0 — 25 miles

front (now it's a gift shop that sells CDs). It was originally a country label, but neighborhood demographics changed and African American musicians began drifting in. The unique combination of gospel, country and blues formed what became soul music. You can walk through the guts of the recording studio, and enjoy splashy displays for Albert King, the Staple Singers and the great Isaac Hayes, the headliner of the 1972 Wattstax festival, the label's high-water mark. Eventually the label went under, but it is now on a campus of the Soulsville Foundation that includes the Stax Music Academy, a public charter school.

The Drive » Head back across town on the I-240N, take the Union Ave exit and head west.

- - - - - - - - - - -

❸ Sun Studio & Graceland (p94)

Sun Studio is where the rockabilly dynasty of Jerry Lee Lewis, Johnny Cash, Roy Orbison and, of course, the King himself (who started here in 1953), was born. Today packed 40-minute guided tours through the tiny studio offer a chance to hear original tapes of historic recording sessions. Guides spin yarns while you pose for photos in the old recording studio on the

'X' where Elvis once stood. Afterwards, hop on the free shuttle to Graceland. Though born in Mississippi, Elvis Presley was a true son of Memphis: raised in the Lauderdale Courts public housing projects, and inspired by the blues in the Beale St clubs, in the spring of 1957 the already-famous 22-year-old spent $100,000 on a Colonial-style mansion, named Graceland by its previous owners. Priscilla Presley (who divorced Elvis in 1973) opened Graceland to tours in 1982, and now millions come here to pay homage to the King and gawk at the infamous decor.

The Drive » Take the I-240 east to the Bill Morris Pkwy, which will take you out of town. Take the TN-57 east from there for about 52 miles, paralleling the Mississippi border. Head north on TN-22 to the Shiloh National Military Park.

- - - - - - - - - - -

❹ Shiloh National Military Park (p100)

Located just north of the Mississippi border near the town of Crump, TN, **Shiloh National Military Park** (www.nps.gov/shil; 1055 Pittsburg Landing Rd; ⏱ park dawn-dusk, visitor center 8am-5pm) reveals the drama behind one of the early major battles of the Civil War. Ulysses S Grant, then a major general, led the Army of Tennessee. After a vicious Confederate assault on

the first day that took Grant by surprise, his creative maneuver on the second day held Pittsburgh Landing, and turned the Confederates back. A relative unknown at the beginning of the war, Grant went on to lead the Union to victory and eventually became the 18th president of the United States. The vast park can only be seen by car. Sights along the route include the Shiloh National Cemetery, the final resting place of 4000 soldiers, an overlook of the Cumberland River where Union reinforcement troops arrived by ship, and various markers and

Shiloh National Military Park Shiloh National Cemetery

monuments. The visitor center gives out maps, shows a video about the battle, and sells an audio driving tour.

The Drive » Continue down the Tennessee back roads, and make your way north on TN-22 to TN-15 east. The road jogs so be conscious of signage. After about 45 miles, turn left on TN-50 east which leads into TN-55 east toward Lynchburg.

- - - - - - - - - - -

TRIP HIGHLIGHT

⑤ Jack Daniel's Distillery (p101)

Set in tiny Moore County (the smallest in Tennessee) is the state's most famous product, **Jack Daniel's Tennessee Whiskey** (www.jackdaniels.

com; 182 Lynchburg Hwy, Lynchburg; ☺9am-4:30pm). And strange gets stranger when you consider it's also a dry county and has been since the soulless scourge of prohibition. Yes, 90 years later dry counties still exist in the South. But, being the South, contradiction is en vogue and you can and will sip a thimble (or more) of the good stuff after the Tasting Tour, which includes an hour-and-a-quarter ramble through the inner workings of the distillery. These enhanced tours are the only type that include a tipple other than lemonade. They are only available a few

times a day, Monday through Saturday, and cost $10. It's best to book ahead. Free tours, usually without a tasting, are offered daily on the hour and are available on a first come, first served basis. The distillery itself sells no memorabilia, so if you want some Old No 7 trinkets, visit the **Lynchburg Hardware & General Store** (51 Mechanic St; ☺9am-5pm Mon-Fri, from 1pm Sun) in town – which is actually owned by the distillery.

The Drive » It's an easy hour-and-a-half drive, mostly off the major interstate, to Nashville. Take TN-55 east to TN-82 north to TN-10 south until you merge with I-24 north for the final 32 miles.

6 Downtown Nashville (p100)

For country-music fans and wannabe songwriters all over the world, a trip to Nashville is the ultimate pilgrimage. Think of any song involving a pick-up truck, a bottle of booze, a no-good woman or a late, lamented hound dog, and the chances are it came from Nashville. Downtown is where you'll find the lion's share of the honky-tonks, as well as the excellent Country Music Hall of Fame (p101), where Elvis' gold Cadillac and Johnny Cash's guitar are enshrined like religious relics. Visit it on our walking tour (p110). Over on Broadway – the heart and soul of the downtown strip – be sure to duck into **Hatch Show Print** (www.hatchshowprint. com; 224 5th Ave S; ⊙9:30am-5pm). For 130 years this classic Nashville printer has been block printing publicity posters. It gets orders from all over the world, and you can buy reprints of original Louis Armstrong, Hank Williams and Bill Monroe shows past.

For music in the present make your way to **Robert's Western World** (www.robertswesternworld. com; 416 Broadway; ⊙11am-2am). Name another dive where you can buy boots, have a burger, a beer or something stronger and listen to a rockabilly band for free all day, every day. **Tootsie's Orchid Lounge** (☏615-726-7937; www .tootsies.net; 422 Broadway; admission free; ⊙10am-late) is equally appealing: a torn-up linoleum-floor dive bar drenched with boot-stomping, hillbilly, beer-soaked grace.

The Drive >> Nashville sprawls a bit, so you will want to drive between downtown and areas south and west. The gridlike streets make it relatively easy to get around.

7 South of Downtown and The West End (p102)

Nashville sprawls a bit, and within the shadow of the downtown skyline are a number of can't-miss clubs and sights for music lovers. Our favorite club in town is the Station Inn (p108). Sit at one of the small cocktail tables, all squeezed together on the worn wood floor, in this beer-only dive. There is no haunt more momentarily famous than **Bluebird Cafe** (☏615-383-1461; www.bluebirdcafe.com; 4104 Hillsboro Rd; cover free-$20; ⊙shows 6pm & 9pm, book ahead). Set in a strip mall in suburban South Nashville, some of the best original singer-songwriters in country music have graced this tiny stage (Steve Earle, Emmylou Harris and the Cowboy Junkies included), which is how it became the central location in the popular television series, *Nashville*. Also in a strip mall, yet still a legit cultural force, is renowned author Anne Patchett's **Parnassus Books** (www.parnassusbooks .net; 3900 Hillsboro Pike; ⊙10am-8pm Mon-Sat, noon-5pm Sun), arguably one of America's most famous indie booksellers. The bright space hosts special

---

MEMPHIS IN MAY

You've heard of Coachella, you've heard of New Orleans Jazz Fest and you may have heard of Bonnaroo, but Memphis' **Beale Street Music Festival** (www.memphisinmay.org; Tom Lee Park; 3-day pass $95; ⊙1st weekend in May) gets very little attention, though it offers one of the country's best line-ups of old-school blues masters, up-and-coming rockers and gloriously past-their-prime pop and hip-hop artists. It runs over three days and attracts 100,000 people to Tom Lee Park each May. No, the Beale Street Festival is not actually on Beale St.

events, readings and signings, promotes local authors, and even sells ebooks. Little nuggets of independence like this may just save our literary souls.

The most famous sight on this end of town is **Music Row** (Music Sq W & Music Sq E), a stretch of 16th and 17th Aves, and home to the production companies, agents, managers and promoters who run Nashville's country-music industry. There's not much to see, but you can pay to cut your own record at some of the smaller studios.

The Drive >> Take the I-40 east to the TN-155 north and watch for the signs. You really can't miss it.

---

8 Grand Ole Opry (p108)

Starting as a radio hour in 1925, country music's signature star-making broadcast operated out of the legendary **Ryman Auditorium** (☎info 615-889-3060, tickets 615-458-8700; www.ryman.com; 116 5th Ave) from 1943 to 1974 before moving out here to the suburbs. After a brief run as a doomed theme park, these days Opryland is a splashy, labyrinthine resort and shopping mall (complete with IMAX theater), but the signature sight remains the **Grand Ole Opry House** (☎615-871-6779; www.opry.com; 2802 Opryland Dr; tours adult/child $22/17; ☺tours 9am-4pm), a modern brick building that seats 4400 for shows. Guided backstage tours are offered daily by reservation – book online up to two weeks ahead. Across the plaza, a small, free museum tells the story of the Opry with wax characters, colorful costumes and dioramas.

DETOUR: FRANKLIN

Start 6 Downtown Nashville

Although it's just 10 miles outside of Nashville, it's worth stopping in the tiny historical hamlet of Franklin. The Victorian-era downtown is charming and the nearby artsy enclave of **Leiper's Fork** is fun and eclectic. But you're in the area to check out one of the Civil War's bloodiest battlefields. On November 30, 1864, 37,000 men (20,000 Confederates and 17,000 Union soldiers) fought over a 2-mile stretch of Franklin's outskirts. Nashville's sprawl has turned much of that battlefield into suburbs, but the **Carter House** (☎615-791-1861; www.carter-house.org; 1140 Columbia Ave; adult/child $15/8; ☺9am-5pm Mon-Sat, 11am-5pm Sun; 👫) property is a preserved chunk of the Battle of Franklin. The house is still riddled with 1000-plus bullet holes.

Historical Mississippi

4

Over the course of her history, Mississippi has proven to be beautiful and wild, serene and violent, complex yet simple. To explore her turbulent past is to discover Mississippi now.

TRIP HIGHLIGHTS

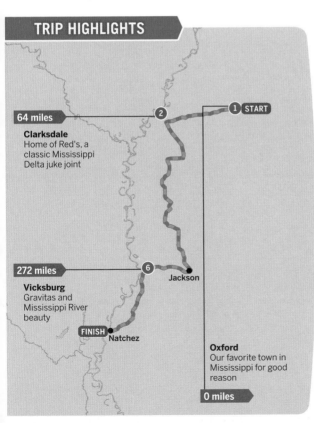

64 miles

Clarksdale
Home of Red's, a classic Mississippi Delta juke joint

272 miles

Vicksburg
Gravitas and Mississippi River beauty

FINISH Natchez

Jackson

Oxford
Our favorite town in Mississippi for good reason

0 miles

START

**3 DAYS
354 MILES / 570KM**

GREAT FOR

BEST TIME TO GO

September and October for a respite from the summer heat; April to June for fresh blooms.

ESSENTIAL PHOTO

The gorgeous grounds of Rowan Oak.

BEST FOR HISTORY

The entire route, from Indian mounds and the birth of the blues to the civil rights movement.

Mississippi River Paddle boat

RAYMOND PATRICK/GETTY IMAGES ©

4 Historical Mississippi

Stroll in the footsteps of literary masters and civil rights heroes, consider the origins of American popular music, and hear gun shots ring and crosses burn in the mind as you stroll blood-soaked battlefields and consider segregation's once-impenetrable stranglehold on the state. Her history will never be easy to reconcile, but her stories – her people – are forever compelling.

TRIP HIGHLIGHT

1 Oxford (p112)

Oxford is one of those rare towns that seeps into your bones and never leaves. Local life revolves around the quaint-yet-hip square, where you'll find inviting bars, wonderful food, decent shopping, and the rather regal **University of Mississippi** (www.olemiss .edu), aka Ole Miss. All around and in between are quiet residential streets, sprinkled with

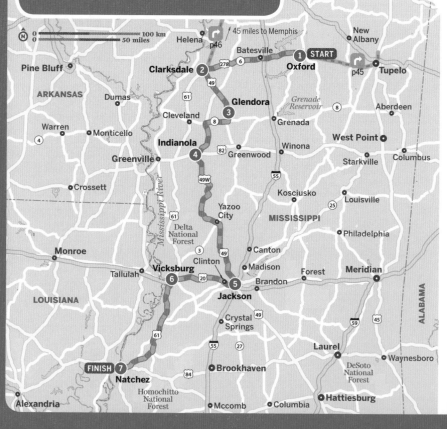

antebellum homes and shaded by majestic oaks. Oh, and there's history to spare. Begin at The Grove, the heart of Ole Miss, and home to one of the Civil Rights movement's iconic scenes. The **Center for Southern Culture archive** (☎662-915-5855; 1 Library Loop; admission free; ⊙8am-9pm Mon-Thu, to 4pm Fri, to 5pm Sat, 1-5pm Sun; ♿), on the 3rd floor of the JD Williams Library, displays William Faulkner's correspondence along with his 1950 Nobel Prize. A half-mile trail leads from the **University of Mississippi Museum** (www.museum.olemiss .edu; University Ave, at 5th St; admission $5; ⊙10am-6pm Tue-Sat), where you'll find a collection of early astronomical marvels, Choctaw lacrosse sticks, Confederate soldier gear, and original Man Ray and Georgia O'Keeffe canvases, through the woods to **Rowan Oak** (www.rowanoak.com; Old Taylor Rd; admission $5; ⊙10am-4pm Tue-Sat, 1-4pm Sun, to 6pm Jun-Aug). This 33-acre estate is the former home of Faulkner. Ninety per cent of the original furnishings are intact, including his prized typewriter. For more on Rowan Oak, see (p112).

The Drive >> It's just over an hour east on MS-6/US 278 through rolling hills into Clarksdale and the Delta.

DETOUR: TUPELO & CONFEDERATE GRAVESITES

Start: ❶ Oxford

A 50-mile detour takes you to Tupelo, which is world famous as **Elvis Presley's birthplace** (www. elvispresleybirthplace.com; 306 Elvis Presley Dr; adult/child $16/7; ⊙9am-5pm Mon-Sat, 1-5pm Sun). The humble building that Elvis lived in as a boy is a pilgrimage site for those who kneel before the king.

Just north of town, on a small rise overlooking the Old Trace, lies a row of 13 graves of unknown Confederate soldiers. What led to their fate has been lost in time, but some theorise that they died during the Confederate retreat from Corinth, Mississippi, following the legendary **Battle of Shiloh**. Others believe they were wounded in the nearby **Battle of Brices Cross Roads**, and buried by their brothers, here. Today they rest as reminders of the ultimate cost of war in any time and place.

CIVIL WAR TRAIL **4** HISTORICAL MISSISSIPPI

TRIP HIGHLIGHT

❷ Clarksdale (p114)

You can't explore Mississippi history without paying homage to the birthplace of American music. Blues legend Robert Johnson is said to have sold his soul to the devil down at **the Crossroads**, the junction of Hwy 61, the Blues Highway, and Hwy 49 in Clarksdale. Clarksdale is the hub of Delta blues country and its most comfortable and vibrant base. Here you can visit Muddy Water's childhood cabin at the Delta Blues Museum (p114), and see modern-day blues men howl at Red's (p115). WC Handy was the first songwriter who finally put the 12-bar blues down on paper, several years after he first heard a nomadic guitar man strumming in tiny Tutwiler in 1903. Their convergence is remembered with a mural along the Tutwiler Tracks (p115).

The Drive >> From Clarksdale, take Hwy 49 south for 13 miles to 49 east, which diverges from 49 west for 13 miles, though both run north and south. Yes, it's confusing, but 16 miles later you will land in Glendora.

❸ Glendora

Sixteen miles south of Tutweiler is another small Delta town, but Glendora's legacy is much darker. It was here on August 28, 1955, that Emmett Till was kidnapped and murdered following a brief encounter with a white woman in a local store. Born in Chicago and just 13 years old, he was ignorant of the local racial mores, and supposedly said, 'Bye Baby,' to a white woman on a dare. Days later he was murdered by the woman's husband and half brother-in-law who were swiftly acquitted of the crime, though there was never an argument as to whether they did it. After Till's mother ordered an open casket at his funeral, so all could see how badly he had been beaten, his case became national news, and a rallying cry for civil rights activists throughout the South. You can learn more about the case at the **Emmett Till Museum** (☎662-375-9304; www.glendorams.com/cultural-heritage-tourism/emmett-till-museum; 33 Thomas St; admission $5; ☻10am-5pm Mon-Fri, to 2pm Sat), which also has a wing dedicated to local

blues legend and BB King's mentor, Sonny Boy Williamson.

The Drive » Take Hwy 49E south for 8 miles to MS-8 west to Hwy 49W, which runs south through the plains until it intersects with Hwy 82 in Indianola.

- - - - - - - - - - - -

④ Indianola (p115)

Indianola is a rather prosperous middle-class town in the Delta with a corporate bloom on Hwy 82, and wide, lovely leafy streets dotted with well-kept single family homes around downtown, where BB King used to play guitar for passers-by. BB King is Indianola's favorite son; you'll see his likeness on murals, and on a plaque on his favorite street corner, and you'll learn all about his difficult, triumphant life at the brand new BB King Museum and Delta Interpretive Center (p115). The region's very best museum offers engaging interactive exhibits that illuminate the various

musical influences on the Delta blues sound, and on King's music in particular. It's a must see for music geeks.

The Drive » Drive south on US 49 to Jackson.

- - - - - - - - - - - -

⑤ Jackson (p116)

Mississippi's capital and largest city has plenty of history to explore, and the **Old Capitol Museum** (www.mdah.state.ms.us/museum; 100 State St; ☻9am-5pm Tue-Sat, 1-5pm Sun) is a good place to start. It tells the story of the Greek Revival building itself, and in so doing touches on Mississippi history. You'll learn that 15 lawmakers opposed secession in the run-up to the Civil War, and there are some interesting exhibits on reconstruction and what were the nation's harshest 'Black Codes,' the gateway to full segregation.

The **Mississippi Museum of Art** (www.msmuseumart.org; 380 South Lamar St; permanent collections free, special exhibitions $5-12; ☻10am-5pm Tue-Sat, noon-5pm Sun) includes 200 works from Mississippi artists. Our favorites are the photographs of literary scions Eudora Welty and William Faulkner, and another of Quincy Jones and Elvis crooning at a Tupelo concert. Housed in Mississippi's first public school for African American kids

DETOUR: MEMPHIS

Start: ② **Clarksdale**

Easily accessible from both Oxford and Clarksdale, Memphis is a thriving city with a blues history to match Mississippi's. Set right on the river, the city's musical roots here (Stax Record, Sun Studios, Graceland) are what attract the tourists, but the warmth and hospitality of the locals is why you'll fall in like or love.

Vicksburg Vicksburg National Military Park cemetery

is the **Smith Robertson Museum** (www.jacksonms.gov/visitors/museums/smithrobertson; 528 Bloom St; adult/child $5/2; ⏰9am-5pm Mon-Fri, 10am-1pm Sat), the alma mater of author Richard Wright. It offers insight into the pain and perseverance of the African American legacy in Mississippi. And then there's the Eudora Welty House (p117), a must for literature buffs.

The Drive ❯❯ It's 44 quick miles west from Jackson to Vicksburg on I-20.

TRIP HIGHLIGHT

❻ Vicksburg (p116)

Vicksburg is famous for its strategic location in the Civil War, thanks to its position on a high bluff overlooking the Mississippi River, and history buffs dig it. General Ulysses S Grant besieged the city for 47 days, until its surrender on July 4, 1863, at which point the North gained dominance over the USA's greatest river.

The **Vicksburg National Military Park** (www.nps.gov/vick; Clay St; per car/individual $8/4; ⏰8am-5pm) honors that battle. You can drive, or pedal (if you're traveling with bicycles), along the 16-mile **Battlefield Drive**, which winds past 1330 monuments and markers – including statues, battle trenches, a restored Union gunboat and a National Cemetery.

Vicksburg's historical riverside core is rather

pretty, and worth a look. You'll find regal old homes lined up on terraced bluffs with views of slender wooded islands and natural inlets, which loom at arm's length along with riverboat casinos.

As long as you're downtown don't miss the **Attic Gallery** (📞601-638-9221; www.atticgallery.net; 1101 Washington St; 🕙10am-5pm Mon-Sat). It features virtuoso regional artists, and a funky collection of folk art and jewelry.

The Drive » Hop on US 61, which follows the Mississippi River (though not always so closely) down to Natchez.

7 Natchez (p119)

Adorable Natchez stews together a wide variety of humans, from gay log-cabin Republicans to intellectual liberals and down-home folks. Perched on a bluff overlooking the Mississippi, it attracts tourists in search of antebellum history and architecture – 668 antebellum homes pepper the oldest civilized settlement on the Mississippi River (beating New Orleans by two years). Although most such towns were torched by Union troops, Natchez was spared thanks to what legend has it were some rather hospitable local ladies who invited the troops in for rest and relaxation. The **visitor and welcome center** (📞601-446-6345; www.visitnatchez.org; 640 S Canal St; tours adult/child $12/8; 🕙8:30am-5pm Mon-Sat, 9am-4pm Sun) is a large, well-organized tourist resource with little exhibits of area history and a ton of information on local sites. During the 'pilgrimage' seasons in spring and fall, local mansions are opened to visitors, though some properties, such as the **Auburn Mansion** (📞601-446-6631; www.natchezpilgrimage.com; Duncan Park; 🕙11am-3pm Tue-Sat, last tour 2:30pm; 👪), are open year-round. Natchez is also the end (or is it the beginning?) of the scenic 444-mile Natchez Trace Pkwy.

Destinations

Washington, DC & the Capital Region (p52)

The nation's capital is an exciting, international city, where world-class sights vie for attention.

Virginia & West Virginia (p72)

Discover a region rich in history and natural beauty.

South Carolina (p82)

Here you will find antebellum architecture, military history and loads of southern charm.

Tennessee (p92)

From the home of Elvis to Nashville's glitting honky-tonks, this state is a music-lover's paradise.

Mississippi (p112)

Located in the heart of the old Confederacy, Mississippi is a fascinating and often misunderstood destination.

Illinois Memorial, Vicksburg National Military Park (p116)
RICHARD CUMMINS/GETTY IMAGES ©

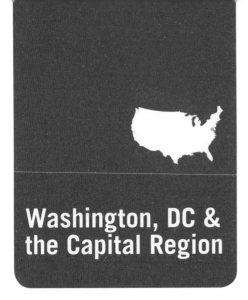

No matter your politics, it's hard not to fall for the nation's capital. Iconic monuments, vast museums and venerable restaurants serving global cuisines are just the beginning of the great DC experience.

Washington, DC & the Capital Region

WASHINGTON, DC

The USA's capital teems with iconic monuments, vast museums and the corridors of power where visionaries and demagogues roam. But it's more than that. It's also home to tree-lined neighborhoods and groovy markets, with ethnically diverse restaurants, large numbers of immigrants and a dynamism percolating just beneath the surface. There's always a buzz here – no surprise, as DC gathers more overachieving and talented types than any city of this size deserves.

Plan on jam-packed days sightseeing in the countless museums (most of them free). At night, join the locals sipping DC-made brews and chowing in cozy restaurants in buzzy quarters such as U St and Logan Circle.

⊙ Sights

Be prepared for big crowds from late March through July, and for sticky-hot days June through August.

⊙ National Mall

When you imagine Washington, DC, you likely imagine this 1.9-mile-long lawn: anchored at one end by the Lincoln Memorial; at the other by Capitol Hill; intersected by the Reflecting Pool and WWII Memorial; and centered on the Washington Monument. This is the heart of the city, and in some ways, of the American experiment itself.

Perhaps no other symbol has so well housed the national ideal of massed voices affecting radical change – from Martin Luther King Jr's 1963 'I Have a Dream' speech to marches for marriage equality in the 2000s. Hundreds of rallies occur here every year: the Mall, framed by great monuments and museums, and shot through with tourists, dog walkers and idealists, acts as a loudspeaker for any cause.

★**Lincoln Memorial**   MONUMENT
(www.nps.gov/linc; 2 Lincoln Memorial Circle NW; ⊙24hr; 🚌 Circulator, Ⓜ Foggy Bottom-GWU) **FREE**
Anchoring the Mall's west end is the hallowed shrine to Abraham Lincoln, who gazes peacefully across the Reflecting Pool beneath his neoclassical Doric-columned abode. To the left of Lincoln you can read the words of the Gettysburg Address, and the hall below highlights other great Lincoln-isms; on the steps, Martin Luther King Jr delivered his famed 'I Have a Dream' speech.

★**Vietnam Veterans Memorial**   MONUMENT
(www.nps.gov/vive; 5 Henry Bacon Dr NW; ⊙24hr; 🚌 Circulator, Ⓜ Foggy Bottom-GWU) **FREE** The opposite of DC's white, gleaming marble is this black, low-lying 'V,' an expression of the psychic scar wrought by the Vietnam War. The monument follows a descent into the earth, with the names of 58,272 dead soldiers – listed in the order in which they died – chiseled into the dark wall. It's a subtle, but profound monument – and all the more

surprising as it was designed by 21-year-old undergraduate student Maya Lin in 1981.

★**Washington Monument** MONUMENT
(www.nps.gov/wamo; 2 15th St NW; ⊘9am-5pm, to 10pm Jun-Aug; ⬚Circulator, ⓂSmithsonian) **FREE** Just peaking at 555ft (and 5in), the Washington Monument is the tallest building in the district. It took two phases of construction to complete; note the different hues of the stone. A 70-second elevator ride whisks you to the observation deck for the city's best views. Same-day tickets for a timed entrance are available at the **kiosk** (15th St, btwn Madison Dr NW & Jefferson Dr SW; ⊘from 8:30am) by the monument. Arrive early.

★**National Air & Space Museum** MUSEUM
(☑202-633-1000; www.airandspace.si.edu; cnr 6th St & Independence Ave SW; ⊘10am-5:30pm, to 7:30pm mid-Mar–early Sep; ⬝; ⬚Circulator, ⓂL'Enfant Plaza) **FREE** The Air and Space Museum is one of the most popular Smithsonian museums. Everyone flocks to see the Wright brothers' flyer, Chuck Yeager's Bell X-1, Charles Lindbergh's *Spirit of St Louis*, Amelia Earhart's natty red plane and the Apollo Lunar Module. An IMAX theater, planetarium and flight simulators are all here ($7 to $9 each). More avionic pieces reside in Virginia at the Steven F Udvar-Hazy Center, an annex holding this museum's leftovers.

★**United States Holocaust Memorial Museum** MUSEUM
(☑202-488-0400; www.ushmm.org; 100 Raoul Wallenberg Pl SW; ⊘10am-5:20pm, to 6:20pm Mon-Fri Apr & May; ⓂSmithsonian) **FREE** For a deep understanding of the Holocaust – its victims, perpetrators and bystanders – this harrowing museum is a must-see. The main exhibit gives visitors the identity card of a single Holocaust victim, whose story is revealed as you take a winding route into a hellish past marked by ghettos, rail cars and death camps. It also shows the flip side of human nature, documenting the risks many citizens took to help the persecuted.

National Gallery of Art MUSEUM
(☑202-737-4215; www.nga.gov; Constitution Ave NW, btwn 3rd & 7th Sts; ⊘10am-5pm Mon-Sat, 11am-6pm Sun; ⬚Circulator, ⓂArchives) **FREE** This staggering collection spans the Middle Ages to the present. The neoclassical west building showcases European art through the early 1900s; highlights include a da Vinci painting and a slew of impressionist and post-impressionist works. The IM Pei–designed

WASHINGTON, DC FACTS

Nickname DC, the District, Chocolate City

Population 659,000

Area 68.3 sq miles

Capital city Exactly!

Sales tax 5.75%

Birthplace of Duke Ellington (1899–1974), Marvin Gaye (1939–84), Dave Chappelle (b 1973)

Home of The Redskins, cherry blossoms, American government

Politics Democrat

Famous for National symbols, crime, partying interns, struggle for Congressional recognition

Unofficial motto and license-plate slogan Taxation Without Representation

East Building displays modern art, with works by Picasso, Matisse and Pollock, and a massive Calder mobile over the entrance lobby. Alas, it's closed (except for the lobby) until fall 2016 for renovations. A trippy underground walkway connects the two wings.

National Sculpture Garden GARDENS
(cnr Constitution Ave NW & 7th St NW; ⊘10am-7pm Mon-Thu & Sat, 10am-9:30pm Fri, 11am-7pm Sun; ⬚Circulator, ⓂArchives) **FREE** The National Gallery of Art's 6-acre garden is studded with whimsical sculptures such as Roy Lichtenstein's *House*, a giant Claes Oldenburg typewriter eraser and Louise Bourgeois' leggy *Spider*. They are scattered around a fountain – a great place to dip your feet in summer. From November to March the fountain becomes a festive **ice rink** (adult/child $8/7, skate rental $3).

In summer, the garden hosts free evening jazz concerts on Fridays from 5pm to 8:30pm.

National Museum of Natural History MUSEUM
(www.mnh.si.edu; cnr 10th St & Constitution Ave NW; ⊘10am-5:30pm, to 7:30pm Jun-Aug; ⬝; ⬚Circulator, ⓂSmithsonian) **FREE** Smithsonian museums don't get more popular than this one, so crowds are pretty much guaranteed. Wave to Henry, the elephant who guards the rotunda, then zip to the 2nd floor's Hope Diamond. The 45.52-carat bauble has cursed its owners, including Marie Antoinette, or so

the story goes. The beloved dinosaur hall is under renovation until 2019, but the giant squid (1st floor, Ocean Hall) and tarantula feedings (2nd floor, Insect Zoo) fill in the thrills at this kid-packed venue.

National Museum of American History
MUSEUM

(www.americanhistory.si.edu; cnr 14th St & Constitution Ave NW; ⊘10am-5:30pm; 🚹; 🚊Circulator, ⓂSmithsonian) FREE This museum collects all kinds of artifacts of the American experience. The centerpiece is the flag that flew over Fort McHenry in Baltimore during the War of 1812 – the same flag that inspired Francis Scott Key to pen *The Star-Spangled Banner*. Other highlights include Julia Child's kitchen (1st floor, Food exhibition), Dorothy's ruby slippers and a piece of Plymouth Rock (both on the 2nd floor, American Stories exhibition).

National Museum of African American History and Culture
MUSEUM

(www.nmaahc.si.edu; 1400 Constitution Ave NW; ⊘10am-5:30pm; 🚊Circulator, ⓂSmithsonian, Federal Triangle) FREE This most recent addition to the Smithsonian fold covers the diverse African American experience and how it helped shape the nation. The collection includes everything from Harriet Tubman's hymnal to Emmett Till's casket to Louis Armstrong's trumpet. The institution is constructing a brand-spankin' new building for the museum, to open in fall 2016. In the

meantime, find exhibits from the collection on show at the next-door National Museum of American History (on the 2nd floor).

National WWII Memorial
MONUMENT

(www.nps.gov/wwii; 17th St; ⊘24hr; 🚊Circulator, ⓂSmithsonian) FREE Dedicated in 2004, the WWII memorial honors the 400,000 Americans who died in the conflict, along with the 16 million US soldiers who served between 1941 and 1945. The plaza's dual arches symbolize victory in the Atlantic and Pacific theaters. The 56 surrounding pillars represent each US state and territory. Stirring quotes speckle the monument. You'll often see groups of veterans paying their respects.

Hirshhorn Museum
MUSEUM

(www.hirshhorn.si.edu; cnr 7th St & Independence Ave SW; ⊘10am-5:30pm; 🚹; 🚊Circulator, ⓂL'Enfant Plaza) FREE The Smithsonian's cylindrical modern art museum stockpiles sculptures and canvases from modernism's early days to pop art to contemporary art. Special exhibits ring the 2nd floor. Rotating pieces from the permanent collection circle the 3rd floor, where there's also a swell sitting area with couches, floor-to-ceiling windows and a balcony offering Mall views.

Smithsonian Castle
NOTABLE BUILDING

(📞202-633-1000; www.si.edu; 1000 Jefferson Dr SW; ⊘8:30am-5:30pm; 🚊Circulator, ⓂSmithsonian) James Renwick designed this turreted red-sandstone fairy tale in 1855. Today the

Smithsonian Castle

castle houses the Smithsonian Visitors Center, which makes a good first stop on the Mall. Inside you'll find history exhibits, multilingual touch-screen displays, a staffed information desk, free maps, a cafe – and the tomb of James Smithson, the institution's founder. His crypt lies inside a little room by the main entrance off the Mall.

Freer-Sackler Museums of Asian Art
MUSEUM

(www.asia.si.edu; cnr Independence Ave & 12th St SW; ◷10am-5:30pm; 🚋Circulator, Ⓜ Smithsonian) FREE This is a lovely spot in which to while away a Washington afternoon. Japanese silk scrolls, smiling Buddhas, rare Islamic manuscripts and Chinese jades spread through cool, quiet galleries. The Freer and Sackler are actually separate venues, connected by an underground tunnel. The Sackler focuses more on changing exhibits, while the Freer, rather incongruously, also houses works by American painter James Whistler. Don't miss the blue-and-gold, ceramics-crammed Peacock Room.

Like all Smithsonian institutions, the venues host free lectures, concerts and film screenings, though the ones here typically have an Asian bent; the website has the schedule. Alas, the Freer is closed for structural renovations from January 1, 2016 until summer of 2017. The Sackler will stay open throughout the period.

National Museum of the American Indian
MUSEUM

(www.nmai.si.edu; cnr 4th St & Independence Ave SW; ◷10am-5:30pm; 🚻; 🚋Circulator, ⓂL'Enfant Plaza) FREE Ensconced in honey-colored, undulating limestone, this museum makes a striking architectural impression. Inside it offers cultural artifacts, costumes, video and audio recordings related to the indigenous people of the Americas. Exhibits are largely organized and presented by individual tribes, which provides an intimate, if sometimes disjointed, overall narrative. The 'Our Universes' gallery (on Level 4), about Native American beliefs and creation stories, is intriguing.

⊙ Tidal Basin

It's magnificent to stroll around this constructed inlet and watch the monument lights wink across the Potomac River. The blooms here are loveliest during the Cherry Blossom Festival, the city's annual spring rejuvenation, when the basin bursts into a

WORTH A TRIP

ARLINGTON NATIONAL CEMETERY

Located across the Potomac River in Virginia, but only a mile or so from the Lincoln Memorial, is Arlington National Cemetery (☎877-907-8585; www.arlingtoncemetery.mil; ◷8am-7pm Apr-Sep, to 5pm Oct-Mar; Ⓜ Arlington Cemetery) FREE This well-known attraction is the somber final resting place for more than 400,000 military personnel and their dependents, with veterans of every US war from the Revolution to Iraq. The cemetery is spread over 612 hilly acres. Departing from the visitor center, bus tours are a handy way to visit the cemetery's memorials.

Highlights include the Tomb of the Unknowns, with its elaborate Changing of the Guard ceremony, and the gravesite of John F and Jacqueline Kennedy, marked by an eternal flame.

pink-and-white floral collage. The original trees, a gift from the city of Tokyo, were planted in 1912.

Martin Luther King Jr Memorial
MONUMENT

(www.nps.gov/mlkm; 1850 W Basin Dr SW; ◷24hr; 🚋Circulator, Ⓜ Smithsonian) FREE Opened in 2011, this is the Mall's first memorial dedicated to a nonpresident, as well as the first to an African American. Sculptor Lei Yixin carved the piece. Besides Dr King's image, known as the *Stone of Hope*, there are two blocks behind him that represent the Mountain of Despair. A wall inscribed with King's stirring quotes flanks the statues. It sits in a lovely spot on the banks of the Tidal Basin.

Franklin Delano Roosevelt Memorial
MONUMENT

(www.nps.gov/frde; 400 W Basin Dr SW; ◷24hr; 🚋Circulator, Ⓜ Smithsonian) FREE The 7.5-acre memorial pays tribute to the US's longest-serving president and the era in which he governed. Visitors are taken through four red-granite 'rooms' that narrate FDR's time in office, from the Depression to the New Deal to WWII. The story is told through statuary and inscriptions, punctuated with fountains and peaceful alcoves. It's especially pretty at night, when the marble shimmers in the glossy stillness of the Tidal Basin.

Washington, DC

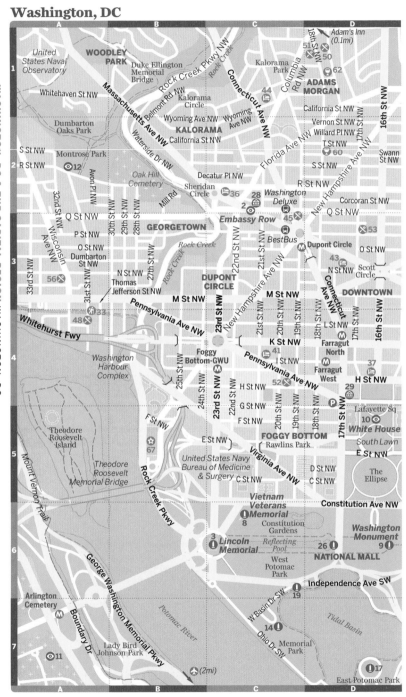

United States Naval Observatory

WOODLEY PARK

Duke Ellington Memorial Bridge

Rock Creek Pkwy NW

Rock Creek

Connecticut Ave NW

Kalorama Park

Columbia Rd NW

62

ADAMS MORGAN

Adam's Inn (0.1mi)

51st St NW

50

18th St NW

Whitehaven St NW

Massachusetts Ave NW

Belmont Rd NW

Kalorama Circle

Wyoming Ave NW

KALORAMA

Waterside Dr NW

California St NW

California St NW

Vernon St NW

Willard Pl NW

T St NW

60

S St NW

California St NW

Florida Ave NW

New Hampshire Ave NW

16th St NW

17th St NW

Swann St NW

Dumbarton Oaks Park

S St NW

R St NW

12

Montrose Park

Oak Hill Cemetery

Avon Pl NW

Mill Rd

Decatur Pl NW

Sheridan Circle

36

28

2

Washington Deluxe

45

R St NW

S St NW

Q St NW

Corcoran St NW

Q St NW

53

32nd St NW

Wisconsin Ave NW

33rd St NW

Q St NW

P St NW

O St NW

Dumbarton St NW

30th St NW

29th St NW

28th St NW

27th St NW

GEORGETOWN

Rock Creek

Embassy Row

BestBus

Dupont Circle

43

N St NW

Scott Circle

O St NW

56

N St NW

Thomas Jefferson St NW

31st St NW

Pennsylvania Ave NW

M St NW

DUPONT CIRCLE

M St NW

22nd St NW

21st St NW

New Hampshire Ave NW

M St NW

Connecticut Ave NW

DOWNTOWN

Whitehurst Fwy

48

33

23rd St NW

21st St NW

20th St NW

19th St NW

18th St NW

17th St NW

16th St NW

K St NW

L St NW

Farragut North

Washington Harbour Complex

Foggy Bottom-GWU

25th St NW

24th St NW

Pennsylvania Ave NW

41

I St NW

Farragut West

H St NW

37

52

29

Theodore Roosevelt Island

F St NW

67

23rd St NW

22nd St NW

H St NW

G St NW

F St NW

20th St NW

19th St NW

18th St NW

17th St NW

P

Lafayette Sq

10

White House

Theodore Roosevelt Memorial Bridge

Rock Creek Pkwy

E St NW

United States Navy Bureau of Medicine & Surgery

Foggy Bottom

Rawlins Park

Virginia Ave NW

South Lawn

E St NW

Mount Vernon Trail

C St NW

D St NW

C St NW

The Ellipse

Vietnam Veterans Memorial

8

Constitution Gardens

Constitution Ave NW

Washington Monument

3

Lincoln Memorial

Reflecting Pool

26

9

West Potomac Park

NATIONAL MALL

Arlington Cemetery

George Washington Memorial Pkwy

Boundary Dr

Lady Bird Johnson Park

11

(2mi)

Potomac River

Independence Ave SW

19

W Basin Dr SW

14

Ohio Dr SW

Memorial Park

Tidal Basin

17

East Potomac Park

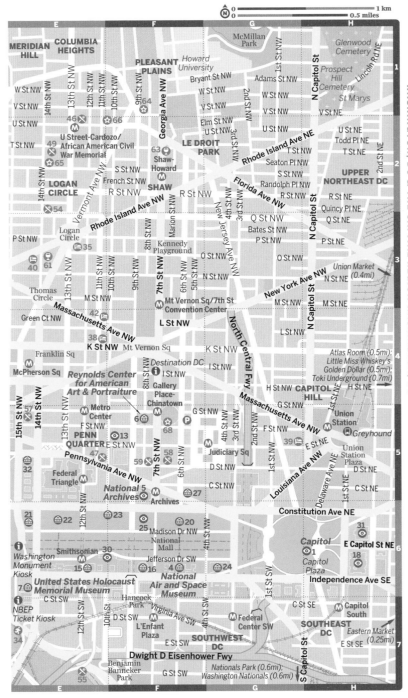

0 1 km
0 0.5 miles

MERIDIAN HILL
COLUMBIA HEIGHTS
PLEASANT PLAINS
Howard University
McMillan Park
Glenwood Cemetery
Prospect Hill Cemetery
St Marys

W St NW
V St NW
U St NW
T St NW

Bryant St NW
Adams St NW
W St NW
V St NW
U St NW

W St NW
V St NW
U St NW
Todd Pl NE
T St NE

Elm St NW
U St NW
T St NW
Seaton Pl NW
S St NW
Randolph Pl NW

U St-Cardozo/African American Civil War Memorial

LE DROIT PARK

UPPER NORTHEAST DC

LOGAN CIRCLE
French St NW
R St NW
SHAW

Rhode Island Ave NE
Florida Ave NW

R St NW
Q St NE
Quincy Pl NE
Q St NE
R St NE

Logan Circle
Kennedy Playground

P St NW
Bates St NW
P St NW

N St NW
O St NW
N St NW

Mt Vernon Sq/7th St Convention Center

Thomas Circle
Green Ct NW
Massachusetts Ave NW

M St NW
L St NW
Mt Vernon Sq
K St NW

Franklin Sq
McPherson Sq
Destination DC
I St NW
Gallery Place-Chinatown

K St NW
I St NW
H St NW
CAPITOL HILL
H St NE

Atlas Room (0.5mi);
Little Miss Whiskey's
Golden Dollar (0.5mi);
Toki Underground (0.7mi)

Union Market (0.4mi)

Reynolds Center for American Art & Portraiture
Metro Center
PENN QUARTER

G St NW
Union Station
Greyhound

Judiciary Sq
F St NW
E St NE

Federal Triangle
Pennsylvania Ave NW
D St NW
Union Station Plaza
D St NE
C St NE

National Archives
Archives

Constitution Ave NE

Madison Dr NW
National Mall

Jefferson Dr SW

Capitol
Capitol Plaza
E Capitol St NE

Washington Monument Kiosk

Smithsonian

National Air and Space Museum

Independence Ave SE

NBEP Ticket Kiosk
United States Holocaust Memorial Museum

C St SW
Hancock Park
Capitol South
SOUTHEAST DC
Eastern Market (0.25mi)

L'Enfant Plaza
Federal Center SW
SOUTHWEST DC

Dwight D Eisenhower Fwy

Benjamin Banneker Park

Nationals Park (0.6mi);
Washington Nationals (0.6mi)

57

Washington, DC

Jefferson Memorial MONUMENT
(www.nps.gov/thje; 900 Ohio Dr SW; ⊙24hr; ☐Circulator, ⓂSmithsonian) FREE Set on the south bank of the Tidal Basin amid the cherry trees, this memorial honors the third US president, political philosopher, drafter of the Declaration of Independence and founder of the University of Virginia. Designed by John Russell Pope to resemble Jefferson's library at the university, the rounded monument was initially derided by critics as 'the Jefferson Muffin.' Inside is a 19ft bronze likeness, and excerpts from Jefferson's writings are etched into the walls.

◎ Capitol Hill

The Capitol, appropriately, sits atop Capitol Hill (we'd say it's more of a stump, but hey), across a plaza from the dignified Supreme

Court and Library of Congress. Congressional office buildings surround the plaza. A pleasant brownstone residential district stretches from E Capitol St to Lincoln Park.

★ Capitol
LANDMARK

(www.visitthecapitol.gov; First St NE & E Capitol St; ⊙8:30am-4:30pm Mon-Sat; Ⓜ Capitol South) **FREE** Since 1800 this is where the legislative branch of American government – ie Congress – has met to write the country's laws. The lower House of Representatives (435 members) and upper Senate (100) meet respectively in the south and north wings of the building. Enter via the underground visitor center below the East Plaza. Guided tours of the building are free, but you need a ticket. Get one at the information desk, or reserve online in advance (there's no fee).

Library of Congress
LIBRARY

(www.loc.gov; 1st St SE; ⊙8:30am-4:30pm Mon-Sat; Ⓜ Capitol South) **FREE** The world's largest library – 29 million books and counting – awes in both scope and design. The centerpiece is the 1897 Jefferson Building. Gawk at the Great Hall, done up in stained glass, marble and mosaics of mythical characters, the Gutenberg Bible (c 1455), Thomas Jefferson's round library and the reading-room viewing area. Free tours of the building take place between 10:30am and 3:30pm on the half-hour.

Supreme Court
LANDMARK

(☏202-479-3030; www.supremecourt.gov; 1 1st St NE; ⊙9am-4:30pm Mon-Fri; Ⓜ Capitol South) **FREE** The highest court in the USA sits in a pseudo-Greek temple that you enter through 13,000lb bronze doors. Arrive early to watch arguments (periodic Monday through Wednesday, October to April). You can visit the permanent exhibits and the building's five-story marble-and-bronze spiral staircase year-round. On days when court is not in session you can also hear lectures (every hour on the half-hour) in the courtroom.

⊙ White House Area & Foggy Bottom

An expansive park called the Ellipse borders the Mall; on the east side is the power-broker block of Pennsylvania Ave. Foggy Bottom was named for the mists that belched out of a local gasworks; now home to the State Department and George Washington University, it's an upscale (if not terribly lively) neighborhood crawling with students and professionals.

★ White House
LANDMARK

(☏tours 202-456-7041; www.whitehouse.gov; ⊙tours 7:30-11:30am Tue-Thu, to 1:30pm Fri & Sat; Ⓜ Federal Triangle, McPherson Sq, Metro Center) **FREE** The White House has survived both fire (the Brits torched it in 1814) and insults (Jefferson groused that it was 'big enough for two emperors, one Pope and the grand Lama'). Tours must be arranged in advance. Americans must apply via one of their state's members of Congress, and non-Americans must apply through either the US consulate in their home country or their country's consulate in DC. Applications are taken from 21 days to six months in advance; three months ahead is the recommended sweet spot.

White House Visitor Center
MUSEUM

(☏202-208-1631; www.nps.gov/whho; 1450 Pennsylvania Ave NW; ⊙7:30am-4pm; Ⓜ Federal Triangle) **FREE** Getting inside the White House can be tough, so here is your backup plan. Browse artifacts such as Roosevelt's desk for his fireside chats and Lincoln's cabinet chair. Multimedia exhibits give a 360-degree view into the White House's rooms. It's not the same as seeing the real deal first-hand, but the center does do its job very well, giving good history sprinkled with great anecdotes on presidential spouses, kids, pets and dinner preferences..

⊙ Downtown

This neighborhood bustles day and night, and several major sights are located here. It's also DC's theater district and convention hub.

★ National Archives
LANDMARK

(☏866-272-6272; www.archives.gov/museum; 700 Pennsylvania Ave NW; ⊙10am-5:30pm Sep–mid-Mar, to 7pm mid-Mar–Aug; Ⓜ Archives) **FREE** It's hard not to feel a little in awe of the big three documents in the National Archives: the Declaration of Independence, the Constitution and the Bill of Rights, plus one of four copies of the Magna Carta. Taken together, it becomes clear just how radical the American experiment was for its time. The Public Vaults, a bare scratching of archival bric-a-brac, make a flashy rejoinder to the main exhibit.

★ Reynolds Center for American Art & Portraiture
MUSEUM

(☏202-633-1000; www.americanart.si.edu; cnr 8th & F Sts NW; ⊙11:30am-7pm; Ⓜ Gallery Pl) **FREE** If you only visit one art museum in DC, make it the Reynolds Center, which combines the

National Mall

Folks often call the Mall 'America's Front Yard,' and that's a pretty good analogy. It is indeed a lawn, unfurling scrubby green grass from the Capitol west to the Lincoln Memorial. It's also America's great public space, where citizens come to protest their government, go for scenic runs and connect with the nation's most cherished ideals writ large in stone, landscaping, monuments and memorials.

You can sample quite a bit in a day, though it'll be a full one that requires roughly 4 miles of walking. Start at the **Vietnam Veterans Memorial ❶**, then head counterclockwise around the Mall, swooping in on the **Lincoln Memorial ❷**, **Martin Luther King Jr Memorial ❸** and **Washington Monument ❹**. You can also pause for the cause of the Korean War and WWII, among other monuments that dot the Mall's western portion.

Martin Luther King Jr Memorial

Walk all the way around the towering statue of Dr King by Lei Yixin and read the quotes. His likeness, incidentally, is 11ft taller than Lincoln and Jefferson in their memorials.

Smithsonian Castle

Seek out the tomb of James Smithson, the eccentric Englishman whose 1826 financial gift launched the Smithsonian Institution. His crypt is in a room by the Mall entrance.

National Air & Space Museum

Simply step inside and look up, and you'll be impressed. Lindbergh's *Spirit of St Louis* and Chuck Yeager's sound barrier–breaking Bell X-1 are among the machines hanging from the ceiling.

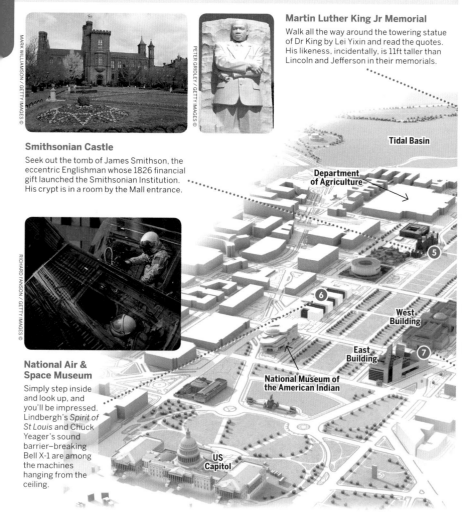

Tidal Basin

Department of Agriculture

West Building

East Building

National Museum of the American Indian

US Capitol

Then it's onward to the museums, all fabulous and all free. Begin at the **Smithsonian Castle ❺** to get your bearings – and to say thanks to the guy making all this awesomeness possible – and commence browsing through the **National Air & Space Museum ❻**, **National Gallery of Art & National Sculpture Garden ❼** and **National Museum of Natural History ❽**.

Lincoln Memorial

Commune with Abe in his chair, then head down the steps to the marker where Martin Luther King Jr gave his 'Dream' speech. The view of the Reflecting Pool and Washington Monument is one of DC's best.

STEVEN GREAVES /GETTY IMAGES ©

Korean War Veterans Memorial

National WWII Memorial

Vietnam Veterans Memorial

Check the symbol that's beside each name. A diamond indicates 'killed, body recovered.' A plus sign indicates 'missing and unaccounted for.' There are approximately 1200 of the latter.

National Museum of African American History & Culture

National Museum of American History

Washington Monument

As you approach the obelisk, look a third of the way up. See how it's slightly lighter in color at the bottom? Builders had to use different marble after the first source dried up.

National Museum of Natural History

Wave to Henry, the elephant who guards the rotunda, then zip to the 2nd floor's Hope Diamond. The 45.52-carat bauble has cursed its owners, including Marie Antoinette, or so the story goes.

National Sculpture Garden

EDDIE BRADY / GETTY IMAGES ©

National Gallery of Art & National Sculpture Garden

Beeline to Gallery 6 (West Building) and ogle the Western Hemisphere's only Leonardo da Vinci painting. Outdoors, amble amid whimsical sculptures by Miró, Calder and Lichtenstein. Also check out IM Pei's design of the East Building.

National Portrait Gallery and the American Art Museum. There is, simply put, no better collection of American art in the world than at these two Smithsonian museums. Famed works by Edward Hopper, Georgia O'Keeffe, Andy Warhol, Winslow Homer and loads more celebrated artists fill the galleries.

Ford's Theatre
HISTORIC SITE

(☑ 202-426-6924; www.fords.org; 511 10th St NW; ☺ 9am-4:30pm; Ⓜ Metro Center) **FREE** On April 14, 1865, John Wilkes Booth assassinated Abraham Lincoln in his box seat here. Timed-entry tickets let you see the flag-draped site. They also provide entry to the basement museum (displaying Booth's .44-caliber pistol, his muddy boot etc) and to Petersen House (across the street), where Lincoln died. Arrive early because tickets do run out. Reserve online ($6.25 fee) to ensure admittance.

Newseum
MUSEUM

(www.newseum.org; 555 Pennsylvania Ave NW; adult/child $23/14; ☺ 9am-5pm; ♿; Ⓜ Archives, Judiciary Sq) This six-story, highly interactive news museum is worth the admission price. You can delve into the major events of recent years (the fall of the Berlin Wall, September 11, Hurricane Katrina), and spend hours watching moving film footage and perusing Pulitzer Prize–winning photographs. The concourse level displays FBI artifacts from news stories, such as the Unabomber's cabin and John Dillinger's death mask.

◉ Dupont Circle

A well-heeled splice of the gay community and the DC diplomatic scene, this is city life at its best. Great restaurants, bars, bookstores and cafes, captivating architecture and the electric energy of a lived-in, happening neighborhood make Dupont worth a linger. Most of the area's historic mansions have been converted into embassies.

★ Embassy Row
ARCHITECTURE

(www.embassy.org; Massachusetts Ave NW btwn Observatory & Dupont Circles NW; Ⓜ Dupont Circle) How quickly can you leave the country? It takes about five minutes; just stroll north along Massachusetts Ave from Dupont Circle (the actual traffic circle) and you pass more than 40 embassies housed in mansions that range from elegant to imposing to discreet. Technically they're on foreign soil, as embassy grounds are the embassy nation's territory.

Phillips Collection
MUSEUM

(www.phillipscollection.org; 1600 21st St NW; Sat & Sun $10, Tue-Fri free, ticketed exhibitions per day $12; ☺ 10am-5pm Tue, Wed, Fri & Sat, to 8:30pm Thu, 11am-6pm Sun, chamber-music series 4pm Sun Oct-May; Ⓜ Dupont Circle) The first modern-art museum in the country (opened in 1921) houses a small but exquisite collection of European and American works. Renoir's *Luncheon of the Boating Party* is a highlight, along with pieces by Gauguin, Van Gogh, Matisse, Picasso and many other greats. The intimate rooms, set in a restored mansion, put you unusually close to the artworks. The permanent collection is free on weekdays.

◉ Georgetown

Thousands of the bright and beautiful, from Georgetown students to ivory-tower academics and diplomats, call this leafy, aristocratic neighborhood home. At night, chockablock M St becomes congested with traffic, a weird mix of high-school cruising and high-street boutique.

Dumbarton Oaks
GARDENS, MUSEUM

(www.doaks.org; 1703 32nd St NW; museum free, gardens adult/child $8/5; ☺ museum 11:30am-5:30pm Tue-Sun, gardens 2-6pm) The mansion's 10 acres of enchanting formal gardens are straight out of a storybook. In springtime, the blooms – including heaps of cherry blossoms – are stunning. The mansion itself is worth a walk-through to see exquisite Byzantine and pre-Columbian art (including El Greco's *The Visitation*), and the fascinating library of rare books.

◉ Anacostia

The drive from Georgetown eastbound to Anacostia takes about 30 minutes – and the patience to endure a world of income disparity. The neighborhood's poverty in contrast to the Mall, sitting mere miles away, forms one of DC's (and America's) great contradictory panoramas. Some high-end condos have sprung up around Nationals Park, the baseball stadium for the Washington Nationals.

Yards Park
PARK

(www.yardspark.org; 355 Water St SE; ☺ 7am-2hr past sunset; Ⓜ Navy Yard) The riverside green space is just down the road from the Nationals' stadium. There are shaded tables by the water, a wooden boardwalk, fountains and a funky modernist bridge that looks like a giant, open-faced plastic straw. Look left and you'll see ships docked at the Navy Yard. Several new restaurants and an excellent brewery at the park's edge ensure you won't hunger or thirst.

Frederick Douglass National Historic Site
HISTORIC SITE

(877-444-6777; www.nps.gov/frdo; 1411 W St SE; ⊙9am-5pm Apr-Oct, to 4:30pm Nov-Mar; Ⓜ Anacostia to bus B2) **FREE** Escaped slave, abolitionist, author and statesman Frederick Douglass occupied this beautifully sited hilltop house from 1878 until his death in 1895. Original furnishings, books, photographs and other personal belongings paint a compelling portrait of both the private and public life of this great man. Keep an eye out for his wire-rim eyeglasses on his rolltop desk. Visits into the home – aka Cedar Hill – are by guided tour only.

🏃 Activities

Hiking & Cycling

C&O Canal Towpath
WALKING, CYCLING

(www.nps.gov/choh; 1057 Thomas Jefferson St NW) The shaded hiking-cycling path – part of a larger national historic park – runs alongside a waterway constructed in the mid-1800s to transport goods all the way to West Virginia. Step on at Jefferson St for a lovely green escape from the crowd.

In its entirety, the gravel path runs for 185 miles from Georgetown to Cumberland, MD. Lots of cyclists do the 14-mile ride from Georgetown to Great Falls, MD. The tree-lined route goes over atmospheric wooden bridges and past waterwheels and old lock houses. It's mostly flat, punctuated by occasional small hills. The park's website and Bike Washington (www.bikewashington.org/canal) have trail maps.

Boating

Tidal Basin Boathouse
BOATING

(www.tidalbasinpaddleboats.com; 1501 Maine Ave SW; 2-/4-person boats $14/22; ⊙10am-6pm mid-Mar–Aug, Wed-Sun only Sep–mid-Oct, closed mid-Oct–mid-Mar; 🚌Circulator, Ⓜ Smithsonian) It rents paddleboats to take out on the Tidal Basin. Make sure you bring a camera. There are great views, of the Jefferson Memorial in particular, from the water.

👉 Tours

DC by Foot
WALKING TOUR

(www.dcbyfoot.com) Guides for this pay-what-you-want walking tour offer engaging stories and historical details on different jaunts covering the National Mall, Lincoln's assassination, Georgetown's ghosts, U Street's food and much more. Most takers pay around $10 per person.

⭐ Festivals & Events

National Cherry Blossom Festival
CULTURAL

(www.nationalcherryblossomfestival.org; ⊙late Mar–early Apr) DC at its prettiest.

The White House (p59)

Smithsonian Folklife Festival　CULTURAL
(www.festival.si.edu; ☉ Jun & Jul) This fun family event, held over two weekends in June and July, features distinctive regional folk art, crafts, food and music.

Independence Day　CULTURAL
(☉ Jul 4) Not surprisingly, a big deal here, celebrated on July 4 with a parade, an open-air concert and fireworks over the Mall.

🛏 Sleeping

Lodging is expensive in DC. The high-season apex is mid-March through April (cherry-blossom season). Crowds and rates also peak in May, June, September and October. Hotel tax adds 14.5% to rates. If you have a car, figure on $35 to $55 per day for in-and-out privileges. Airbnb can also be a good option in the city. For B&Bs and private apartments citywide, contact **Bed & Breakfast DC** (www.bedandbreakfastdc.com).

🛏 Capitol Hill

Hotel George　BOUTIQUE HOTEL $$
(☎ 202-347-4200; www.hotelgeorge.com; 15 E St NW; r from $300; P ❧ ❄ @ ☎ ☀; M Union Station) DC's first chic boutique hotel is still one of its best. Chrome-and-glass furniture and modern art frame the bold interior. Rooms exude a cool, creamy-white Zen. The pop-art presidential accents (paintings of American currency, artfully rearranged and diced up) are a little overdone, but that's a minor complaint about what is otherwise the hippest lodging on the Hill.

🛏 Downtown & White House Area

Hostelling International – Washington DC　HOSTEL $
(☎ 202-737-2333; www.hiwashingtondc.org; 1009 11th St NW; dm $33-55, r $110-150; ❧ ❄ @ ☎; M Metro Center) Top of the budget picks, this large, friendly hostel attracts a laid-back international crowd and has loads of amenities: lounge rooms, a pool table, a 60in TV for movie nights, free tours, free continental breakfast and free wi-fi.

★**Hotel Lombardy**　BOUTIQUE HOTEL $$
(☎ 202-828-2600; www.hotellombardy.com; 2019 Pennsylvania Ave NW; r $180-330; P ❧ ❄ @ ☎; M Foggy Bottom-GWU) Done up in Venetian decor (shuttered doors, warm gold walls), and beloved by World Bank and State De-

partment types, this European boutique hotel has multilingual staff and an international vibe – you hear French and Spanish as often as English in its halls. The attitude carries into rooms decorated with original artwork and Chinese and European antiques.

Morrison-Clark Inn　HISTORIC HOTEL $$
(☎ 202-898-1200; www.morrisonclark.com; 1015 L St NW; r $150-250; P ❧ ❄ @ ☎; M Mt Vernon Sq) Listed on the National Register of Historic Places and helmed by a doting staff, the elegant Morrison-Clark comprises two 1864 Victorian residences filled with fine antiques, chandeliers, richly hued drapes and other features evocative of the pre–Civil War South. Some rooms are on the small side, but more options are coming: the inn is expanding into a church next door.

★**Hay-Adams Hotel**　HERITAGE HOTEL $$$
(☎ 202-638-6600; www.hayadams.com; 800 16th St NW; r from $350; P ❄ @ ☎ ☀; M McPherson Sq) One of the city's great heritage hotels, the Hay is a beautiful old building where 'nothing is overlooked but the White House.' The property has a palazzo-style lobby and probably the best rooms of the old-school, luxury genre in the city, all puffy mattresses like clouds shaded by four-poster canopies and gold-braid tassels.

🛏 U Street, Shaw & Logan Circle

Hotel Helix　BOUTIQUE HOTEL $$
(☎ 202-462-9001; www.hotelhelix.com; 1430 Rhode Island Ave NW; r $200-300; P ❧ ❄ @ ☎ ☀; M McPherson Sq) Modish and highlighter bright, the Helix is playfully hip – the perfect hotel for the bouncy international set that makes up the surrounding neighborhood. Little touches suggest a youthful energy (Pez dispensers in the minibar) balanced with worldly cool (like the pop-punk decor). All rooms have comfy, crisp-sheet beds and 37in flat-screen TVs.

Chester Arthur House　B&B $$
(☎ 877-893-3233; www.chesterarthurhouse.com; 23 Logan Circle NW; r $175-215; ❧ ❄ ☎; M U St) Snooze in one of four rooms in this beautiful Logan Circle row house, located a stumble from the restaurant boom along P and 14th Sts. The 1883 abode is stuffed with crystal chandeliers, antique oil paintings and a mahogany-paneled staircase, plus ephemera from the hosts' global expeditions.

📮 Adams Morgan

Adam's Inn B&B $
(☎ 202-745-3600; www.adamsinn.com; 1746 Lanier Pl NW; r $109-179, without bathroom $79-100; P ⊖ ❋ @ 🛜; M Woodley Park) Tucked on a shady residential street, the 26-room inn is known for its personalized service, fluffy linens and handy location just a few blocks from 18th St's global smorgasbord. Inviting, homey rooms sprawl through two adjacent townhouses and a carriage house. The common areas have a nice garden patio, and there's a general sense of sherry-scented chintz.

Taft Bridge Inn B&B $$
(☎ 202-387-2007; www.taftbridgeinn.com; 2007 Wyoming Ave NW; r $179-205, without bathroom $100-140; P ⊖ ❋ 🛜; M Dupont Circle) Named for the bridge that leaps over Rock Creek Park just north, this beautiful 19th-century Georgian mansion is an easy walk to 18th St or Dupont Circle. The inn has a paneled drawing room, classy antiques, six fireplaces and a garden. Some of the 12 rooms have a Colonial Americana theme, accentuated by Amish quilts; others are more tweedy, exuding a Euro-Renaissance vibe.

📮 Dupont Circle

★ Tabard Inn BOUTIQUE HOTEL $$
(☎ 202-785-1277; www.tabardinn.com; 1739 N St NW; r $195-250, without bathroom $135-155; ⊖ ❋ @ 🛜; M Dupont Circle) Named for the inn in *The Canterbury Tales,* the Tabard spreads through a trio of Victorian-era row houses. The 40 rooms are hard to generalize: all come with vintage quirks such as iron bed frames and wing-backed chairs, though little accents distinguish – a Matisse-like painted headboard here, Amish-looking quilts there. There are no TVs, and wi-fi can be dodgy, but the of-yore atmospherics prevail.

Continental breakfast is included. Downstairs the parlor, beautiful restaurant and bar have low ceilings and old furniture, highly conducive to curling up with a vintage port and the Sunday *Post.*

Embassy Circle Guest House B&B $$
(☎ 202-232-7744; www.dcinns.com; 2224 R St NW; r $180-300; ⊖ ❋ 🛜; M Dupont Circle) Embassies surround this 1902 French country–style home, which sits a few blocks from Dupont's nightlife hubbub. The 11 big-windowed rooms are decked out with Persian carpets and original art on the walls; they don't have

TVs or radios, though they do each have wifi. Staff feeds you well throughout the day, with a hot organic breakfast, afternoon cookies, and an evening wine and beer soiree.

🍴 Eating

Washington's dining scene is booming. The number of restaurants has doubled over the past decade, with small, independent spots helmed by local chefs leading the way. There's also a delicious glut of global cuisines and traditional Southern fare.

🍴 Capitol Hill

This hood has two particularly rich veins for eating and drinking. You'll find 8th St SE (near Eastern Market) – also known as Barracks Row – packed with venues. So is H St NE, an edgy corridor a mile east of Union Station; catch bus X2 or a taxi (about $8). The District's long-awaited streetcars might be rolling there soon, as well.

Toki Underground ASIAN $
(☎ 202-388-3086; www.tokiunderground.com; 1234 H St NE; mains $10-12; ⊙ 11:30am-2:30pm & 5-10pm Mon-Thu, to midnight Fri & Sat; 🚌 X2 from Union Station) Spicy ramen noodles and dumplings sum up wee Toki's menu. Steaming pots obscure the busy chefs, while diners slurp and sigh contentedly. The eatery doesn't take reservations and there's typically a wait. Take the opportunity to explore surrounding bars;

Toki will text when your table is ready. The restaurant isn't signposted; look for the Pug bar, and Toki is above it.

Maine Avenue Fish Market SEAFOOD $
(1100 Maine Ave SW; mains $7-13; ⊗8am-9pm; Ⓜ L'Enfant Plaza) The pungent, open-air Maine Avenue Fish Market is a local landmark. No-nonsense vendors sell fish, crabs, oysters and other seafood so fresh it's almost still flopping. They'll kill, strip, shell, gut, fry or broil your desire, which you can take to the waterfront benches and eat blissfully (mind the seagulls!).

Atlas Room AMERICAN $$
(⌨ 202-388-4020; www.theatlasroom.com; 1015 H St NE; mains $21-25; ⊗5:30-9:30pm Tue-Thu, 5:30-10pm Fri & Sat, 5-9pm Sun; ⌹ X2 from Union Station) Set in a snug room, shimmering with candlelight, Atlas is a neighborhood favorite on edgy H St. The bistro takes cues from classical French and Italian gastronomy but blends them in approachable American ways using seasonal ingredients. In summer you might enjoy crab fritters, while in winter a braised daube of beef will melt your tongue (in a good way!).

✖ Downtown & White House Area

★ Red Apron Butchery DELI $
(⌨ 202-524-5244; www.redapronbutchery.com; 709 D St NW; mains $5-10; ⊗7:30am-8pm Mon-Fri, 9am-8pm Sat, 9am-5pm Sun; Ⓜ Archives) Red Apron makes a helluva breakfast sandwich. Plop into one of the comfy booths and wrap your lips around the ricotta, honey and pinenut 'aristocrat' or the egg and chorizo 'buenos dias.' They're all heaped onto *tigelle* rolls, a sort of Italian flatbread. But you have to order before 10:30am (2:30pm on weekends).

★ Founding Farmers MODERN AMERICAN $$
(⌨ 202-822-8783; www.wearefoundingfarmers. com; 1924 Pennsylvania Ave NW; mains $14-26; ⊗11am-10pm Mon, 11am-11pm Tue-Thu, 11am-midnight Fri, 9am-midnight Sat, 9am-10pm Sun; ⌨; Ⓜ Foggy Bottom-GWU, Farragut West) ⬤ A frosty decor of pickled goods in jars adorns this buzzy dining space. The look is a combination of rustic-cool and modern art that reflects the nature of the food: locally sourced, New American fare. Buttermilk fried chicken and waffles, and zesty pork and lentil stew are a few of the favorites. The restaurant is located in the IMF building.

Rasika INDIAN $$
(⌨ 202-637-1222; www.rasikarestaurant.com; 633 D St NW; mains $14-28; ⊗11:30am-2:30pm Mon-Fri, 5:30-10:30pm Mon-Thu, 5-11pm Fri & Sat; ⌨; Ⓜ Archives) Rasika is as cutting edge as Indian food gets. The room resembles a Jaipur palace decorated by a flock of modernist art-gallery curators. Narangi duck is juicy, almost unctuous, and pleasantly nutty thanks to the addition of cashews; the deceptively simple *dal* (lentils) has the right kiss of sharp fenugreek. Vegans and vegetarians will feel a lot of love here.

Old Ebbitt Grill AMERICAN $$
(⌨ 202-347-4800; www.ebbitt.com; 675 15th St NW; mains $12-22; ⊗7:30am-1am Mon-Fri, from 8:30am Sat & Sun; Ⓜ Metro Center) The Grill has occupied its prime real estate, by the White House, since 1846. Political players (and lots of tourists) pack into the brass and wood interior, the sound of their conversation rumbling across a dining room where thick burgers, crab cakes and fish-and-chip type fare are rotated out almost as quickly as the clientele. Pop in for a drink and oysters during happy hour.

★ Central
Michel Richard MODERN AMERICAN $$$
(⌨ 202-626-0015; www.centralmichelrichard. com; 1001 Pennsylvania Ave NW; mains $19-34; ⊗11:30am-2:30pm Mon-Fri, 5-10:30pm Mon-Thu, 5-11pm Fri & Sat; Ⓜ Federal Triangle) Michel Richard is known for his high-end eating establishments in the District, but Central stands out as a special experience. It's aimed at hitting a comfort-food sweet spot. You're dining in a four-star bistro where the food is old-school favorites with a twist: lobster burgers, a sinfully complex meatloaf and fried chicken that redefines what fried chicken can be.

✖ U Street, Shaw & Logan Circle

★ Ben's Chili Bowl AMERICAN $
(www.benschilibowl.com; 1213 U St; mains $5-10; ⊗6am-2am Mon-Thu, 6am-4am Fri, 7am-4am Sat, 11am-midnight Sun; Ⓜ U St) Ben's is a DC institution. The main stock in trade is half-smokes, DC's meatier, smokier version of the hot dog, usually slathered in mustard, onions and the namesake chili. For nearly 60 years presidents, rock stars and Supreme Court justices have come in to indulge in the humble diner; but, despite the hype, Ben's remains a true neighborhood establishment. Cash only.

Ben's Chili Bowl

★ **Compass Rose** INTERNATIONAL **$$**
(📞202-506-4765; www.compassrosedc.com; 1346 T St NW; small plates $10-15; ⊙5pm-2am Sun-Thu, to 3am Fri & Sat; Ⓜ U St) Compass Rose feels like a secret garden, set in a discreet townhouse a whisker from 14th St's buzz. The exposed brick walls, rustic wood decor and sky-blue ceiling give it a casually romantic air. The menu is a mash-up of global comfort foods, so dinner might entail, say, a Chilean *lomito* (pork sandwich), Lebanese *kefta* (ground lamb and spices) and Georgian *khachapuri* (buttery, cheese-filled bread).

★ **Le Diplomate** FRENCH **$$$**
(📞202-332-3333; www.lediplomatedc.com; 1601 14th St NW; mains $22-31; ⊙5-10pm Mon & Tue, 5-11pm Wed & Thu, 5pm-midnight Fri, 9:30am-midnight Sat, 9:30am-10pm Sun; Ⓜ U St) This charming French bistro is a relative newcomer, but it has skyrocketed to become one of the hottest tables in town. DC celebrities galore cozy up in the leather banquettes and at the sidewalk tables. They come for an authentic slice of Paris, from the *coq au vin* (wine-braised chicken) and aromatic baguettes to the vintage curios and nudie photos decorating the bathrooms. Make reservations.

✖ Adams Morgan

Diner AMERICAN **$**
(www.dinerdc.com; 2453 18th St NW; mains $9-17; ⊙24hr; 👶; Ⓜ Woodley Park-Zoo/Adams Morgan)

The Diner serves hearty comfort food, any time of the day or night. It's ideal for wee-hour breakfast scarf-downs, weekend Bloody-Mary brunches (if you don't mind crowds) or any time you want unfussy, well-prepared American fare. Omelets, fat pancakes, mac 'n' cheese, grilled Portobello sandwiches and burgers hit the tables with aplomb. It's a good spot for kids, too.

★ **Donburi** JAPANESE **$**
(📞202-629-1047; www.facebook.com/donburidc; 2438 18th St NW; mains $9-12; ⊙11am-10pm; Ⓜ Woodley Park-Zoo/Adams Morgan) Hole-in-the-wall Donburi has 15 seats at a wooden counter where you get a front-row view of the slicing, dicing chefs. *Donburi* means 'bowl' in Japanese, and that's what arrives, steaming hot and filled with, say, panko-coated shrimp atop rice and blended with the house's sweet-and-savory sauce. It's a simple, authentic meal. There's often a line, but it moves quickly. No reservations.

✖ Dupont Circle

★ **Afterwords Cafe** AMERICAN **$$**
(📞202-387-3825; www.kramers.com; 1517 Connecticut Ave; mains $15-21; ⊙7:30am-1am Sun-Thu, 24hr Fri & Sat; Ⓜ Dupont Circle) Attached to Kramerbooks, this buzzing spot is not your average bookstore cafe. The packed indoor tables, wee bar and outdoor patio overflow with good cheer. The menu features tasty bistro fare and an ample beer selection, making it a

prime spot for happy hour, for brunch and at all hours on weekends (open 24 hours, baby!).

★ **Little Serow**   THAI $$$
(www.littleserow.com; 1511 17th St NW; fixed menu per person $45; ⊘ 5:30-10pm Tue-Thu, to 10:30pm Fri & Sat; Ⓜ Dupont Circle) Little Serow has no phone, no reservations and no sign on the door. It only seats groups of four or fewer (larger parties will be separated) but, despite all this, people line up around the block. And what for? Superlative northern Thai cuisine. The single-option menu – which consists of six or so hot-spiced courses – changes by the week.

Komi   FUSION $$$
(☑ 202-332-9200; www.komirestaurant.com; 1509 17th St NW; set menu $135; ⊘ 5-9:30pm Tue-Thu, to 10pm Fri & Sat; Ⓜ Dupont Circle) There is an admirable simplicity to Komi's changing menu, which is rooted in Greece and influenced by everything – primarily genius. Suckling pig for two; scallops and truffles; roasted baby goat. Komi's fairytale of a dining space doesn't take groups larger than four, and you need to reserve way in advance – like, now.

✕ Georgetown

★ **Chez Billy Sud**   FRENCH $$
(☑ 202-965-2606; www.chezbillysud.com; 1039 31st St NW; mains $17-29; ⊘ 11:30am-2pm Tue-Fri, 11am-2pm Sat & Sun, 5-10pm Tue-Thu & Sun, 5-11pm Fri & Sat; ☑) An endearing little bistro tucked away on a residential block, Billy's mint-green walls, gilt mirrors and wee marble bar exude laid-back elegance. Mustachioed servers bring baskets of warm bread to the white-linen–clothed tables, along with crackling pork and pistachio sausage, golden trout, tuna nicoise salad and plump cream puffs.

Martin's Tavern   AMERICAN $$
(☑ 202-333-7370; www.martins-tavern.com; 1264 Wisconsin Ave NW; mains $17-32; ⊘ 11am-1:30am Mon-Thu, 11am-2:30am Fri, 9am-2:30am Sat, 8am-1:30am Sun) John F Kennedy proposed to Jackie in booth three at Georgetown's oldest saloon, and if you're thinking of popping the question there today, the attentive waitstaff keep the champagne chilled for that very reason. With an old-English country scene, including the requisite fox-and-hound hunting prints on the wall, this DC institution serves unfussy classics such thick burgers, crab cakes and icy-cold beers.

Drinking & Nightlife

See the free alternative weekly *Washington City Paper* (www.washingtoncitypaper.com) for comprehensive listings. DC is a big happy-hour town – practically all bars have some sort of drink special for a few hours between 4pm and 7pm.

◉ Capitol Hill

★ **Bluejacket Brewery**   BREWERY
(☑ 202-524-4862; www.bluejacketdc.com; 300 Tingey St SE; ⊘ 11am-1am Sun-Thu, to 2am Fri & Sat; Ⓜ Navy Yard) Beer lovers' heads will explode in Bluejacket. Pull up a stool at the mod-industrial bar, gaze at the silvery tanks bubbling up the ambitious brews, then make the hard decision about which of the 25 tap beers you want to try. A dry-hopped kolsch? Sweet-spiced stout? A cask-aged farmhouse ale? Four-ounce tasting pours help with decision-making.

Little Miss Whiskey's Golden Dollar   BAR
(www.littlemisswhiskeys.com; 1104 H St NE; ⊘ 5pm-2am; ☐ X2 from Union Station) If Alice had returned from Wonderland so traumatized by her near-beheading that she needed a stiff drink, we imagine she'd pop down to Little Miss Whiskey's. She'd love the whimsical-meets-dark-nightmares decor. And she'd probably have fun with the club kids partying on the upstairs dance floor on weekends. She'd also adore the weirdly fantastic back patio.

◉ U Street, Shaw & Logan Circle

★ **Right Proper Brewing Co**   BREWERY
(www.rightproperbrewery.com; 624 T St NW; ⊘ 5-11pm Tue-Thu, to midnight Fri & Sat, to 10pm Sun; Ⓜ Shaw-Howard U) As if the artwork – a chalked mural of the National Zoo's giant pandas with laser eyes destroying downtown DC – wasn't enough, Right Proper Brewing Co makes sublime ales in a building where Duke Ellington used to play pool. It's the Shaw district's neighborhood clubhouse, a big, sunny space filled with folks gabbing at reclaimed wood tables.

Churchkey   BAR
(www.churchkeydc.com; 1337 14th St NW; ⊘ 4pm-1am Mon-Thu, 4pm-2am Fri, noon-2am Sat, noon-1am Sun; Ⓜ McPherson Sq) Coppery, mod-industrial Churchkey glows with hipness. Fifty beers flow from the taps, including five brain-walloping, cask-aged ales. If none of those please you, another 500 types of brew are

available by the bottle (including gluten-free suds). Churchkey is the upstairs counterpart to Birch & Barley, a popular nouveau comfort-food restaurant, and you can order much of its menu at the bar.

Dupont Circle & Adams Morgan

★ Dan's Cafe
BAR

(2315 18th St NW; ☺ 7pm-2am Tue-Thu, to 3am Fri & Sat; Ⓜ Woodley Park-Zoo/Adams Morgan) This is one of DC's great dive bars. The interior looks sort of like an evil Elks Club, all un-ironically old-school 'art,' cheap paneling and dim lights barely illuminating the unapologetic slumminess. It's famed for its whopping, mix-it-yourself drinks, where you get a ketchup-type squirt bottle of booze, a can of soda and bucket of ice for barely $20.

Bar Charley
BAR

(www.barcharley.com; 1825 18th St NW; ☺ 5pm-12:30am Mon-Thu, 4pm-1:30am Fri, 10am-1:30am Sat, 10am-12:30am Sun; Ⓜ Dupont Circle) Bar Charley draws a mixed crowd from the neighborhood – young, old, gay and straight. They come for groovy cocktails sloshing in vintage glassware and ceramic tiki mugs, served at very reasonable prices by DC standards. Try the gin and ginger Suffering Bastard. The beer list isn't huge, but it is thoughtfully chosen with some wild ales. Around 60 wines are available, too.

☆ Entertainment

Live Music

Black Cat
LIVE MUSIC

(www.blackcatdc.com; 1811 14th St NW; Ⓜ U St) A pillar of DC's rock and indie scene since the 1990s, the battered Black Cat has hosted all the greats of years past (White Stripes, the Strokes, Arcade Fire and others). If you don't want to pony up for $20-a-ticket bands on the upstairs main stage (or the smaller Backstage below), head to the Red Room for the jukebox, pool and strong cocktails.

9:30 Club
LIVE MUSIC

(www.930.com; 815 V St NW; admission from $10; Ⓜ U St) This place, which can pack 1200 people into a surprisingly compact venue, is the granddaddy of the live music scene in DC. Pretty much every big name that comes through town ends up on this stage, and a concert here is the first-gig memory of many a DC-area teenager. Headliners usually take the stage between 10:30pm and 11:30pm.

Kennedy Center

Bohemian Caverns
JAZZ

(www.bohemiancaverns.com; 2001 11th St NW; admission $7-22; ☺ 7pm-midnight Mon-Thu, 7:30pm-2am Fri & Sat, 6pm-midnight Sun; Ⓜ U St) Back in the day, Bohemian Caverns hosted the likes of Miles Davis, John Coltrane and Duke Ellington. Today you'll find a mix of youthful renegades and soulful legends. Monday night's swingin' house band draws an all-ages crowd.

Performing Arts

Kennedy Center
PERFORMING ARTS

(☎ 202-467-4600; www.kennedy-center.org; 2700 F St NW; Ⓜ Foggy Bottom-GWU) Sprawled on 17 acres along the Potomac River, the magnificent Kennedy Center hosts a staggering array of performances – more than 2000 each year among its multiple venues, including the Concert Hall (home to the National Symphony) and Opera House (home to the National Opera). A free shuttle bus runs to and from the Metro station every 15 minutes from 9:45am (noon on Sunday) to midnight.

Sports

★ Washington Nationals
BASEBALL

(www.nationals.com; 1500 S Capitol St SE; ☎; Ⓜ Navy Yard) The major-league Nats play baseball at Nationals Park beside the Anacostia River. Don't miss the mid-fourth-inning 'Racing Presidents' – an odd foot race between giant-headed caricatures of George Washington, Abraham Lincoln, Thomas Jefferson, Teddy Roosevelt and William Taft. The stadium itself is spiffy, and hip

Gettysburg National Military Park
CRAIG FILDES/GETTY IMAGES ©

eaties and mod Yards Park have cropped up around it as the area gentrifies.

Washington Redskins FOOTBALL
(☑ 301-276-6800; www.redskins.com; 1600 Fedex Way, Landover, MD; Ⓜ Morgan Blvd) Washington's NFL team, the Redskins, plays September through January at FedEx Field. The team has experienced a lot of controversy recently, and not only because of its woeful play. Many groups have criticized the Redskins' name and logo as insulting to Native Americans. The US Patent and Trademark Office agreed, and revoked the team's trademark.

Washington Capitals HOCKEY
(http://capitals.nhl.com; 601 F St NW; Ⓜ Gallery Pl) Washington's rough-and-tumble pro hockey team skates at the Verizon Center from October to April. Tickets start from around $40.

Washington Wizards BASKETBALL
(www.nba.com/wizards; 601 F St NW; Ⓜ Gallery Pl) Washington's winning pro basketball team plays at the Verizon Center from October through April. The lowest-price tickets are around $30 for the nosebleed section, and the cost goes way up from there.

ⓘ Information

Cultural Tourism DC (www.culturaltourismdc. org) Offers a large range of DIY neighborhood walking tours.

Destination DC (☑ 202-789-7000; www. washington.org) DC's official tourism site, with the mother lode of online information.
George Washington University Hospital (☑ 202-715-4000; 900 23rd St NW; Ⓜ Foggy Bottom-GWU)
Washington City Paper (www.washington citypaper.com) Free edgy weekly with entertainment and dining listings.
Washington Post (www.washingtonpost.com) Respected daily city (and national) paper. Its daily tabloid-format *Express* is free.

MARYLAND

The western spine of Maryland is mountain country. The Appalachian peaks soar to 3000ft above sea level, and the surrounding valleys are packed with rugged scenery and Civil War battlefields. This is Maryland's playground, where hiking, skiing, rock climbing and white-water rafting draw the outdoors-loving crowd.

Frederick

Halfway between the battlefields of Gettysburg, PA and Antietam is Frederick; its handsome 50-square-block historic district resembles an almost perfect cliche of a mid-sized city.

⊙ Sights

National Museum of Civil War Medicine MUSEUM
(www.civilwarmed.org; 48 E Patrick St; adult/student/child $9.50/7/free; ⊙10am-5pm Mon-Sat, from 11am Sun) This museum provides a fascinating, and sometimes gruesome, look at the health conditions soldiers and doctors faced during the war, as well as important medical advances that resulted from the conflict.

🍴 Sleeping & Eating

Hollerstown Hill B&B B&B $$
(☑ 301-228-3630; www.hollerstownhill.com; 4 Clarke Pl; r $145-175; Ⓟ ❊ 🛜) The elegant, friendly Hollerstown has four pattern-heavy rooms, two resident terriers and an elegant billiards room. This lovely Victorian sits right in the middle of the historic downtown area of Frederick, so you're within easy walking distance of all the goodness. No children under 16.

Brewer's Alley GASTROPUB **$$**
(☎ 301-631-0089; 124 N Market St; mains $10-26; ⊙ noon-11:30pm; ⃝) This bouncy brewpub is one of our favorite places in Frederick for several reasons. First, the beer: house-brewed, plenty of variety, delicious. Second, the burgers: enormous, half-pound monstrosities of staggeringly yummy proportions. Third, the rest of the menu: excellent Chesapeake seafood (including a wood-fired pizza topped with crab) and Frederick county farm produce and meats.

Cacique LATIN **$$**
(☎ 301-695-2756; 26 N Market Street; $11-29; ⊙ 11:30am-10pm Sun-Thu, to 1:30pm Fri & Sat) This interesting spot mixes up a menu of Spanish favorites, such as paella and tapas, with Latin American gut busters like enchiladas and ceviche. That said, the focus and the expertise seems bent more towards the Iberian side of the menu; the shrimp sauteed in garlic and olive oil is wonderful.

Antietam National Battlefield

The site of the bloodiest day in American history is now, ironically, supremely peaceful, quiet and haunting – uncluttered save for plaques and statues. On September 17, 1862, General Robert E Lee's first invasion of the North was stalled here in a tactical stalemate that left more than 23,000 dead, wounded or missing – more casualties than America had suffered in all her previous wars combined. Poignantly, many of the battlefield graves are inscribed with German and Irish names, a roll call of immigrants who died fighting for their new homeland. The **visitor center** (☎ 301-432-5124; 5831 Dunker Church Road, Sharpsburg; 3-day pass per person/vehicle $5/10; ⊙ 9am-5pm) shows a short film (playing on the hour and half-hour) about the events that transpired here. It also sells books and materials, including self-guided driving and walking tours of the battlefield.

PENNSYLVANIA

More than 300 miles across, stretching from the East Coast to the edge of the Midwest, Pennsylvania contains multitudes. Philadelphia, once the heart of the British colonial empire, is very much a part of the east, a link on the Boston–Washington metro corridor. Out-side the city, though, the terrain turns pastoral, emphasized by the Pennsylvania Dutch – that is, Mennonite, Amish and others – who tend their farms by hand, as if it were still the 18th century. West of here, the Appalachian Mountains begin, as do the so-called Pennsylvania Wilds, a barely inhabited patch of deep forest. In the far west edge of the state, Pittsburgh, the state's only other large city and once a staggeringly wealthy steel manufacturing center, is fascinating in its combination of rust-belt decay and new energy.

Gettysburg

This town 145 miles west of Philadelphia, now quite tranquil and pretty, is synonymous with one of the bloodiest battles of the Civil War. Over three days in July 1863, some 8000 people were killed. Later that year, President Abraham Lincoln delivered his Gettysburg Address ('Four score and seven years ago...'), reinforcing the war's mission of equality.

Gettysburg National Military Park (☎ 717-334-1124; www.nps.gov/gett; 1195 Baltimore Pike; museum adult/child $12.50/8.50, ranger tours per vehicle $65, bus tours adult/child $30/18; ⊙ museum 8am-6pm Apr-Oct, to 5pm Nov-Mar, grounds 6am-10pm Apr-Oct, to 7pm Nov-Mar) covers 8 sq miles of land marked with monuments and trails. The museum at the visitor center is a must-see, for the awe-inspiring cyclorama – a life-size, 360-degree painting – of Pickett's Charge, the especially disastrous battle on the last day. Originally made in 1884, the painting was restored and reinstalled in 2008, with a dramatic light show and narration. Out in the park, you can explore on your own, on a bus tour or – most recommended – on a two-hour ranger-led tour in your own car.

Gettysburg itself is a pretty town, worth spending the night in, but plan ahead in summer, especially in July, when the town is mobbed with battle reenactors. For accommodations, try **Brickhouse Inn** (☎ 717-338-9337; www.brickhouseinn.com; 452 Baltimore St; r from $149; P ※ ⃝), two adjacent old buildings with a lovely back garden; the owners take breakfast so seriously there's even a pie course. **Dobbin House** (☎ 717-334-2100; 89 Steinwehr Ave; sandwiches $10, mains $25; ⊙ tavern 11:30am-9pm, main restaurant from 5pm), built in 1776, is an inn and restaurant. The food is average, but the setting, all candlelit and creaky, is great. The tavern in the basement has a cheaper bar menu, with burgers and soups.

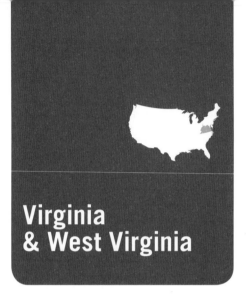

Virginia & West Virginia

Beautiful Virginia is a state steeped in history. It was the birthplace of America, and it has played a lead role in nearly every major American drama since, including the Civil War.

VIRGINIA

Virginia's natural beauty is as diverse as its history and people. Chesapeake Bay and the wide sandy beaches kiss the Atlantic Ocean. Pine forests, marshes and rolling green hills form the soft curves of the central Piedmont region, while the rugged Appalachian Mountains and stunning Shenandoah Valley line its back.

Manassas

On July 21, 1861, Union and Confederate soldiers clashed in the first major land battle of the Civil War. Expecting a quick victory, DC residents flocked here to picnic and watch the First Battle of Bull Run (known in the South as First Manassas). The surprise Southern victory erased any hopes of a quick end to the war. Union and Confederate soldiers again met on the same ground for the larger Second Battle of Manassas in August 1862; again the South was victorious. Today, Manassas National Battlefield Park (p20) is a curving green hillscape, sectioned into fuzzy fields of tall grass and wildflowers by split-rail wood fences. Start your tour at the Henry Hill Visitor Center (📞703-361-1339; ⊙8:30am-5pm) to watch the orientation film and pick up park and trail maps.

✕ Eating

There are several restaurants and bars around the Manassas train station, but the rest of the city is a mess of strip malls and suburban sprawl.

Tandoori Village   INDIAN $$
(📞703-369-6526; 7607 Centreville Road; mains $8-19; ⊙11am-2:30pm & 5-10pm Mon-Fri, 11am-10pm Sat & Sun) Tandoori Village serves up solid Punjabi cuisine, offering a welcome dash of spice and flavor complexity to an area that's pretty rife with fast food chains. No menu shockers here, but all the standards, like butter chicken, dal, paneer and the rest, are executed with competence.

Fredericksburg

Fredericksburg is a pretty town with a historical district that's almost a cliché of small-town Americana. George Washington grew up here, and the Civil War exploded in the streets and surrounding fields. Today the main street is a pleasant amble of bookstores, gastropubs and cafes.

◉ Sights

Fredericksburg & Spotsylvania National Military Park   HISTORIC SITE
(www.nps.gov/frsp) FREE More than 13,000 Americans were killed during the Civil War in four battles fought in a 17-mile radius cov-

ered by this park, today maintained by the NPS (National Park Service). Don't miss the burial site of Stonewall Jackson's amputated arm near the **Fredericksburg Battlefield visitor center** (☑540-373-6122; www.nps.gov/frsp; 1013 Lafayette Blvd; film $2; ☺9am-5pm).

Stonewall Jackson Shrine　MONUMENT
See p21.

**James Monroe Museum
& Memorial Library**　HISTORIC SITE
(☑540-654-1043; http://jamesmonroemuseum.umw.edu; 908 Charles St; adult/child $6/2; ☺10am-5pm Mon-Sat, from 1pm Sun) The museum's namesake was the nation's fifth president. US history nerds will delight in the small curious collection of Monroe memorabilia, including the desk on which he wrote the famous Monroe Doctrine.

Mary Washington House　HISTORIC BUILDING
(☑540-373-5630; 1200 Charles St; adult/child $5/2; ☺11am-5pm Mon-Sat, noon-4pm Sun) At the 18th-century home of George Washington's mother, knowledgeable tour guides in period costume shed light on Mary and what life was like in her time. The lovely garden is an excellent re-creation from the era.

🛏 Sleeping & Eating

You'll find dozens of restaurants and cafes along historic Caroline and William Sts.

Richard Johnston Inn　B&B $$
(☑540-899-7607; www.therichardjohnstoninn.com; 711 Caroline St; r $125-250; P✱☏) In an 18th-century brick mansion, this cozy B&B scores points for location, comfort and friendliness.

Schooler House　B&B $$
(☑540-287-5407; www.theschoolerhouse.com; 1303 Caroline St; r $160-175; P✱) Two lacy bedrooms in a watermelon-colored house with a gorgeous patio and backyard set the scene in this excellent Victorian B&B. The owners are warm and welcoming and cook a mean breakfast to boot. Service is personalized – you feel like these folks really care about your holiday.

Sammy T's　AMERICAN $
(☑540-371-2008; www.sammyts.com; 801 Caroline St; mains $8-14; ☺11:30am-9:30pm; ☏✎) Sammy T's wins points off the bat for its attractive location: a cute brick building constructed circa 1805 in the heart of historic Fredericksburg. The food isn't bad

either, mainly consisting of soup and sandwich, pub-like fare, with an admirable mix of vegetarian options such as a local take on lasagna and black bean quesadillas. There's a good beer selection, too.

Foode　AMERICAN $$
(☑540-479-1370; www.foodeonline.com; 1006C/D Caroline St; mains lunch $9-11, dinner $15-25; ☺11am-3pm & 4.30pm-8pm Tue-Sat, 10am-2pm Sun; ✎) ✿ Foode serves up tasty farm-to-table fare in a rustic but artsy setting.

Bistro Bethem　AMERICAN $$$
(☑540-371-9999; www.bistrobethem.com; 309 William St; mains $19-34; ☺11:30am-2:30pm & 5-10pm Tue-Sat, to 9pm Sun) The New American menu, seasonal ingredients and down-to-earth but dedicated foodie vibe here all equal gastronomic bliss. On any given day duck confit and quinoa may share the table with a roasted beet salad and local clams.

Richmond

Richmond has been the capital of the Commonwealth of Virginia since 1780. It's an old-fashioned Southern city that's grounded in tradition on one hand, but full of income disparities and social tensions on the other. Yet it's an undeniably handsome town, with red-brick row houses, a rushing river and leafy parks.

Its history is ubiquitous and, sometimes, uncomfortable; this was where patriot Patrick Henry gave his famous 'Give me Liberty, or give me Death!' speech, and where the slave-holding Southern Confederate States placed their capital. Today the 'River City' is a surprisingly dynamic place, with a buzzing food-and-drink scene, fascinating neighborhoods and a wide range of attractions.

◉ Sights

Cold Harbor BATTLEFIELD
See p23.

**White House of the
Confederacy** HISTORIC SITE
See p24.

**American Civil War Center
at Historic Tredegar** MUSEUM
(www.tredegar.org; 490 Tredegar St; adult/child $10/8; ⊙9am-5pm) Located in an 1861 gun foundry, this fascinating site explores the causes and course of the Civil War from the perspectives of Union, Confederate and African American experiences. Next door is a free site run by the National Park Service that delves into Richmond's role during the war. This is one of 13 protected area sites that make up Richmond National Battlefield Park (www.nps.gov/rich).

Canal Walk WATERFRONT
(www.rvariverfront.com; btwn 5th and 17th Sts) The 1.25-mile waterfront Canal Walk between the James River and the Kanawha (ka-*naw*) and Haxall Canals is a lovely way of seeing a dozen highlights of Richmond history in one go. There's also a pedestrian bridge across to Belle Isle, a scruffy but intriguing island in the James.

Belle Isle PARK
(www.jamesriverpark.org) A long pedestrian bridge leads from Tredegar St (just past the national park site) out to this car-free island. Once a quarry, power plant and POW camp during the Civil War (though never all at once), today this is one of Richmond's finest city parks. The big flat rocks are lovely for sunbathing, and hiking and biking trails abound – but don't swim in the James River. It's polluted and the currents are treacherous.

Virginia State Capitol BUILDING
(www.virginiacapitol.gov; cnr 9th & Grace Sts, Capitol Sq; ⊙8am-5pm Mon-Sat, 1-5pm Sun) FREE Designed by Thomas Jefferson, the capitol building was completed in 1788 and houses the oldest legislative body in the Western Hemisphere – the Virginia General Assembly, established in 1619. Free tours available.

Virginia Historical Society MUSEUM
(www.vahistorical.org; 428 North Blvd; adult/student $6/4; ⊙10am-5pm Mon-Sat, from 1pm Sun) The VHS is looking grander than ever following a multimillion-dollar renovation. Changing and permanent exhibits trace the history of the Commonwealth from prehistoric to present times.

St John's Episcopal Church CHURCH
(www.historicstjohnschurch.org; 2401 E Broad St; tours adult/child $7/5; ⊙10am-4pm Mon-Sat, from 1pm Sun) It was here that firebrand Patrick Henry uttered his famous battle cry – 'Give me Liberty, or give me Death!' – during the rebellious 1775 Second Virginia Convention. His speech is re-enacted from 1pm to 3pm on Sundays in summer.

Virginia Museum of Fine Arts MUSEUM
(VMFA; ☑804-340-1400; www.vmfa.museum; 200 North Blvd; ⊙10am-5pm Sat-Wed, to 9pm Thu & Fri) FREE Has a remarkable collection of European works and sacred Himalayan art, plus one of the largest Fabergé egg collections on display outside Russia. Also hosts excellent temporary exhibitions (admission ranges from free to $20).

Poe Museum MUSEUM
(☑804-648-5523; www.poemuseum.org; 1914-16 E Main St; adult/student $6/5; ⊙10am-5pm Tue-Sat, from 11am Sun) Contains the world's largest collection of manuscripts and memorabilia of poet Edgar Allan Poe, who lived and worked in Richmond.

Hollywood Cemetery CEMETERY
(☑804-649-0711; www.hollywoodcemetery.org; entrance cnr Albemarle & Cherry Sts; ⊙8am-5pm, to 6pm summer) FREE This tranquil cemetery, perched above the James River rapids, contains the gravesites of two US presidents (James Monroe and John Tyler), the only Confederate president (Jefferson Davis) and 18,000 Confederate soldiers. Free walking tours are given at 10am Monday through Saturday and 2pm on Sunday.

Monument Avenue Statues
STATUE

(btwn N Lombardy St & Roseneath Rd) Monument Ave, a tree-lined boulevard in northeast Richmond, holds statues of such revered Southern heroes as JEB Stuart, Robert E Lee, Matthew Fontaine Maury, Jefferson Davis, Stonewall Jackson and – in a nod to diversity – African American tennis champion Arthur Ashe.

🛏 Sleeping

⭐ HI Richmond
HOSTEL $

(www.hiusa.org; 7 N 2nd St; dm around $30; ❋ 🛜) Inside a historic 1924 building, this new, eco-friendly hostel has a great central location and bright rooms (both dorms and private rooms), with high ceilings and loads of original details. There's a kitchen for guests, inviting common areas, and it's completely accessible for travelers with disabilities.

Massad House Hotel
MOTEL $

(☑ 804-648-2893; www.massadhousehotel.com; 11 N 4th St; r $80-115) Massad's great by any standard, but excellent rates and a supreme location near the heart of Richmond's best attractions give it a special place in our hearts. The design will put you in mind of a cozy study in Tudor-style budget bliss.

Linden Row Inn
BOUTIQUE HOTEL $$

(☑ 804-783-7000; www.lindenrowinn.com; 100 E Franklin St; r $100-190; P ❋ @ 🛜) This antebellum gem has 70 attractive rooms (with period Victorian furnishings) spread among neighboring Greek Revival townhouses in an excellent downtown location. Friendly Southern hospitality and thoughtful extras (free passes to the YMCA, free around-town shuttle service) sweeten the deal.

Museum District B&B
B&B $$

(☑ 804-359-2332; www.museumdistrictbb.com; 2811 Grove Ave; r from $150; P ❋ 🛜) In a fine location near the dining and drinking of Carytown, this stately 1920s brick B&B has earned many admirers for its warm welcome. Rooms are comfortably set and guests can enjoy the wide front porch, cozy parlor with fireplace, and excellent cooked breakfasts – plus wine and cheese in the evenings.

Jefferson Hotel
LUXURY HOTEL $$$

(☑ 804-649-4750; www.jeffersonhotel.com; 101 W Franklin St; r $365; P ❋ 🛜 ☀) The Jefferson is Richmond's grandest hotel and one of the finest in America. The vision of tobacco tycoon and Confederate major Lewis Ginter, the beaux-arts-style hotel was completed in

Jefferson Davis Monument, Monument Avenue
JOSH RINEHULT/GETTY IMAGES ©

1895. According to rumor, the magnificent grand staircase in the lobby served as the model for the famed stairs in *Gone with the Wind*.

Even if you don't stay here, it's worth having a peek inside. If you have time, try the hotel's afternoon tea, served beneath Tiffany stained glass in the Palm Court lobby (from 3pm Friday to Sunday), or have a drink at the grand Lemaire Bar.

🍴 Eating

You'll find dozens of restaurants along the cobbled streets of Shockoe Slip and Shockoe Bottom. Further west in Carytown (W Cary St between S Blvd and N Thompson St) are even more dining options.

⭐ Mama J's
AMERICAN $

(415 N 1st St; mains $7-10; ⊙ 11am-9pm Sun-Thu, to 10pm Fri & Sat) Set in the historic African American neighborhood of Jackson Ward, Mama J's serves up delicious fried chicken and legendary fried catfish, along with collard greens, mac 'n' cheese, candied yams and other fixings. The service is friendly and the lines are long – go early to beat the crowds.

17th Street Farmers Market
MARKET $

(cnr 17th & E Main Sts; ⊙ 8:30am-4pm Sat & Sun) For cheap eats and fresh produce, check out this bustling market, which runs from late April through early October. On Sundays the market sells antiques.

Vegetable stalls at 17th Street Farmers Market (p75)

Sub Rosa BAKERY **$**
(620 N 25th St; pastries $3-5; ⊙ 7am-6pm Tue-Fri, 8:30am-5pm Sat & Sun) In the historic Church Hill neighborhood, Sub Rosa is a wood-fired bakery serving some of the best baked goods in the South.

Kuba Kuba CUBAN **$**
(1601 Park Ave; mains $7-17; ⊙ 9am-9:30pm Mon-Sat, to 8pm Sun) In the Fan district, this tiny hole-in-the-wall feels like a bodega straight out of Old Havana, with mouth-watering roast pork dishes, Spanish-style omelets and panini at rock-bottom prices.

Sidewalk Cafe AMERICAN **$**
(2101 W Main St; mains $9-18; ⊙ 11:30am-2am Mon-Fri, from 9am Sat & Sun) A much-loved local haunt, Sidewalk Cafe feels like a dive bar (year-round Christmas lights, wood-paneled walls, kitschy artwork), but the food is first rate. There's outdoor seating on the sidewalk, daily specials (eg Taco Tuesdays) and legendary weekend brunches.

Burger Bach GASTROPUB **$**
(☑ 804-359-1305; http://theburgerbach.com; 10 S Thompson St; mains $9-14; ⊙ 11am-10pm, to 11pm Fri & Sat; ☑ ☖) We give Burger Bach credit for being the only restaurant found in the area that self-classifies as a New Zealand–inspired burger joint. And that said, why yes, they do serve excellent lamb burgers here, although the locally sourced beef (and vegetarian) options are awesome as well.

You should really go crazy with the 14 different sauces available for the thick-cut fries.

The Daily MODERN AMERICAN **$$**
(☑ 804-342-8990; 2934 W Cary St; mains $10-25; ⊙ 7am-10pm Sun-Thu, to midnight Fri & Sat; ☑) ☚ In the heart of Carytown, the Daily is a great dining and drinking choice no matter the time of day. Stop by for lump crab omelets at breakfast, blackened mahimahi BLT at lunch and seared scallops by night. Extensive vegan options, first-rate cocktails and a buzzing, artfully designed space (complete with dramatically lit trees) seal the deal.

Millie's Diner MODERN AMERICAN **$$**
(☑ 804-643-5512; 2603 E Main St; lunch $9-12, dinner $22-26; ⊙ 11am-2:30pm & 5:30-10:30pm Tue-Fri, 9am-3pm & 5:30-10:30pm Sat & Sun) Lunch, dinner or weekend brunch – Richmond icon Millie's does it all, and does it well. It's a small but handsomely designed space, with creative seasonal fare. The Devil's Mess – an open-faced omelet with spicy sausage, curry, veg, cheese and avocado – is legendary.

Croaker's Spot SEAFOOD **$$**
(☑ 804-269-0464; www.croakersspot.com; 1020 Hull St; mains $13-30; ⊙ 11am-9pm Mon, Tue & Wed, to 10pm Thu, to 11pm Fri & Sat, noon-9pm Sun; ☑) Croaker's is an institution in these parts, a backbone of the African American dining scene. Richmond's most famous rendition of refined soul food is comforting, delicious and sits in your stomach like a brick. Beware

the intimidating Fish Boat: fried catfish, cornbread and mac 'n' cheese.

Boathouse at Rocketts Landing   SEAFOOD $$$
(☑804-622-2628; 4708 E Old Main St; mains $14-32; ☺5pm-midnight Mon-Thu, from 3pm Fri, from noon Sat & Sun) The Boathouse serves good seafood plates (crispy calamari, Chapel Creek oysters, sesame-seared tuna) and pub fare in a fabulous setting overlooking the James River. The breezy deck is also a fine spot for a sundowner. It's located about 1 mile south of Shockoe Bottom.

Edo's Squid   ITALIAN $$$
(☑804-864-5488; 411 N Harrison St; mains $12-35; ☺11am-10pm, from 5:30pm Sun) One of the best Italian restaurants in Richmond, Edo's serves up mouthwatering, authentic cuisine such as eggplant parmesan, spicy shrimp diavolo pasta, daily specials and, of course, squid.

Julep's   MODERN AMERICAN $$$
(☑804-377-3968; 420 E Grace St; mains $23-32; ☺5:30-10pm Mon-Sat; P) This is where classy, old-school Southern aristocrats like to meet and eat, drawn by the fresh experimentation of an innovative kitchen. We were fans of the wild boar and lamb stew, but vegetarian options abound, and the salad menu is creative.

Drinking & Entertainment

Legend Brewing Company   MICROBREWERY
(☑804-232-3446; www.legendbrewing.com; 321 W 7th St; ☺11:30am-11pm Mon-Sat, to 10pm Sun) On the south side of the James River, this place has excellent microbrews, tasty pub grub and fine views of the city from its popular outdoor deck. There's live bluegrass on Sundays (6:30pm), rock and other music on Fridays (8pm), and free brewery tours on Saturdays (1pm).

From downtown, it's a short hop across the bike- and pedestrian-friendly Manchester (S 9th St) Bridge.

Saison   COCKTAIL BAR
(23 W Marshall St; ☺5pm-2am) This classy drinking den attracts serious cocktail lovers, who clink glasses over creative libations, craft beer and farm-to-table fare. It's in Jackson Ward, near downtown.

Capital Ale House   BAR
(623 E Main St; ☺11am-1:30am) Popular with political wonks from the nearby state capitol, this downtown pub has a superb beer selection (more than 50 on tap and 250 bottled) and decent pub grub.

Cary Street Cafe   LIVE MUSIC
(☑804-353-7445; www.carystreetcafe.com; 2631 W Cary St; ☺8am-2am Mon-Fri, from 11am Sat & Sun) Live music (plus the odd karaoke crooner) emanates from this excellent bar just about every night of the week. This spot is proudly prohippie, but doesn't just bust out hippie tunes; the gigs juke from reggae and folk to alt-country and gypsy rock.

Byrd Theater   CINEMA
(☑804-353-9911; www.byrdtheatre.com; 2908 W Cary St; tickets from $2) You can't beat the price at this classic 1928 cinema, which shows second-run films. Wurlitzer-organ concerts precede the Saturday-night shows.

Information
Johnston-Willis Hospital (☑804-330-2000; 1401 Johnston-Willis Dr)
Post Office (700 E Main St; ☺7:30am-5pm Mon-Fri)
Richmond-Times Dispatch (www.richmond.com) Daily newspaper.
Richmond Visitor Center (☑804-783-7450; www.visitrichmondva.com; 405 N 3rd St; ☺9am-5pm)
Style Weekly (www.styleweekly.com) Alternative weekly with listings of events, restaurants, nightlife and the arts.

Petersburg
About 25 miles south of Richmond, the little town of Petersburg played a big role in the Civil War as a major railway junction, transporting Confederate troops and supplies. Union troops laid a 10-month siege of Petersburg in 1864–65, the longest on American soil. The Siege Museum (☑804-733-2404; 15 W Bank St; adult/child $5/4, incl Old Blandford Church $11/9; ☺10am-5pm) relates the plight of civilians during the siege. Several miles east of town, Petersburg National Battlefield (p24) is where Union soldiers planted explosives underneath a Confederate breastwork, leading to the Battle of the Crater (novelized and cinematized in *Cold Mountain*). West of downtown in Pamplin Historical Park, the excellent National Museum of the Civil War Soldier (☑804-861-2408; www.pamplinpark.org; 6125 Boydton Plank Rd; adult/child $13/8; ☺9am-5pm) illustrates the hardships faced by soldiers on both sides of the conflict.

Appomattox Court House & Around

At the McLean House in the town of Appomattox Court House, General Robert E Lee surrendered the Army of Northern Virginia to General Ulysses S Grant, in effect ending the Civil War. Instead of coming straight here, follow Lee's retreat (☎800-673-8732; www.varetreat.com) on a winding, 25-stop tour that starts in Petersburg at Southside Railroad Station (River St and Cockade Alley) and cuts through some of the most attractive countryside in Virginia. Best take a detailed road map, as the trail is not always clearly marked.

You'll finish at the 1700-acre Appomattox Court House National Park (p25). The park comprises over two dozen restored buildings. A number of buildings are open to visitors, and set with original and period furnishings from 1865. Highlights include the parlor of the McLean House, where Lee and Grant met; the Clover Hill Tavern, used by Union soldiers to print 30,000 parole passes for Confederate soldiers; and the dry-goods-filled Meeks General Store.

The town of Appomattox (3 miles southwest of the national park) is small but charming, with a main street dotted with antique shops (a gold mine for hunters of Civil War memorabilia). Stop in at Baine's Books and Coffee (www.bainesbooks.com;

205 Main St; snacks $3-6; ⊙8:30am-8pm Mon-Sat, 9am-5pm Sun) for sandwiches, quiche and scones (plus live bluegrass several nights a week). If you need a place to stay, nearby Longacre (☎800-758-7730; www.longacreva.com; 1670 Church St; r from $105; P❄) looks as if it got lost somewhere in the English countryside and decided to set up shop in Virginia. Its elegant rooms are set with antiques, and lush grounds surround the sprawling Tudor-style house.

WEST VIRGINIA

Wild and wonderful West Virginia is often overlooked by both American and foreign travelers. It doesn't help that the state can't seem to shake its negative stereotypes. That's too bad, because West Virginia is one of the prettiest states in the Union. With its line of unbroken green mountains, raging white-water rivers and snowcapped ski resorts, this is an outdoor-lovers' paradise.

Created by secessionists from secession, the people here still think of themselves as hardscrabble sons and daughters of miners, and that perception isn't entirely off. But the Mountain State is also gentrifying and, occasionally, that's a good thing: the arts are flourishing in the valleys, where some towns offer a welcome break from the state's constantly evolving outdoor activities.

STEVE HEAP/SHUTTERSTOCK ©

Clover Hill Tavern, Appomattox Court House National Historic Park

Harpers Ferry

History lives on in this attractive town, set with steep cobblestoned streets, framed by the Shenandoah Mountains and the confluence of the rushing Potomac and Shenandoah Rivers. The lower town functions as an open-air museum, with more than a dozen buildings that you can wander through to get a taste of 19th-century small-town life. Exhibits narrate the town's role at the forefront of westward expansion, American industry and, most famously, the slavery debate – in 1859 old John Brown tried to spark a slave uprising here and was hanged for his efforts; the incident rubbed friction between North and South into the fires of Civil War.

Pick up a pass to visit the historic buildings at the **Harpers Ferry National Historic Park Visitor Center** (☑304-535-6029; www.nps.gov/hafe; 171 Shoreline Dr; per person/vehicle $5/10; ⊙9am-5pm; ⊕) ✐ off Hwy 340. You can also park and take a free shuttle from here. Parking is extremely limited in Harpers Ferry proper.

◉ Sights

You can freely enter over a dozen buildings that are part of the **Harpers Ferry National Historic Park**. Start your exploring at the information center on Shenandoah St, near the riverfront. From there, you can pick up a map and stroll into nearby buildings, all of which offer a unique perspective on life in the past.

Black Voices   MUSEUM
(High St; ⊙9am-5pm) **FREE** This worthwhile, interactive exhibit has narrated stories of African American hardships and hard-won victories from the times of enslavement through the Civil Rights era. Across the street is the Storer College exhibit, which gives an overview of the groundbreaking educational center and the Niagara movement that formed in its wake.

John Brown Museum   MUSEUM
(Shenandoah St; ⊙9am-5pm) **FREE** Across from Arsenal Sq, this three-room gallery gives a fine overview (through videos and period relics) of the events surrounding John Brown's famous raid.

Master Armorer's House   HISTORIC SITE
(☑304-535-6029; www.nps.gov/hafe; Shenandoah St; ⊙9am-5pm) **FREE** One of the free sites in the historic district, this 1858 house explains

how rifle technology developed here went on to revolutionize the firearms industry.

Storer College Campus   HISTORIC SITE
(www.nps.gov/hafe; Fillmore St) Founded immediately after the Civil War, Storer College grew from a one-room schoolhouse for freed slaves to a respected college open to all races and creeds. It closed in 1955. You can freely wander the historic campus, reachable by taking the path to upper town, past St Peter's church, Jefferson Rock and Harper Cemetery.

John Brown Wax Museum   MUSEUM
(☑304-535-6342; www.johnbrownwaxmuseum. com; 168 High St; adult/child $7/5; ⊙9am-4:30pm, 10am-5:30pm summer, limited hours winter) Not to be confused with the National Park–run museum, this private wax museum is a kitschy (and rather overpriced) attraction that pays tribute to the man who led an ill-conceived slave rebellion here. The exhibits are laughably old-school; nothing says historical accuracy like scratchy vocals, jerky animatronics and dusty old dioramas.

⚡ Activities

There are great hiking trails in the area, from three-hour scrambles to the scenic overlook from the Maryland Heights Trail, past Civil War fortifications on the Loudoun Heights Trail or along the Appalachian Trail. You can also cycle or walk along the C&O Canal towpath.

Appalachian Trail Conservancy HIKING
(☎304-535-6331; www.appalachiantrail.org; cnr Washington & Jackson Sts; ☺9am-5pm) The 2160-mile Appalachian Trail is headquartered here at this tremendous resource for hikers.

River Riders ADVENTURE SPORTS
(☎800-326-7238; www.riverriders.com; 408 Alstadts Hill Rd) The go-to place for rafting, canoeing, tubing, kayaking and multiday cycling trips, plus cycle rental. There's even a new 1200ft zip line.

O Be Joyfull WALKING TOUR
(☎732-801-0381; www.obejoyfull.com; 175 High St; day/night tours $22/14) Offers eye-opening historical daytime walking tours (lasting three to four hours) around Harpers Ferry, as well as a spooky 90-minute evening tour.

🛏 Sleeping

Teahorse Hostel HOSTEL $
(☎304-535-6848; www.teahorsehostel.com; 1312 Washington St; dm/ste $33/150; P❄@🗘) Popular with cyclists on the C&O Canal towpath and hikers on the Appalachian Trail, Teahorse is a welcoming place with comfy rooms and common areas (including an outdoor patio). It's located 1 mile (uphill) from the historic lower town of Harpers Ferry.

HI-Harpers Ferry Hostel HOSTEL $
(☎301-834-7652; www.hiusa.org; 19123 Sandy Hook Rd, Knoxville, MD; dm/d $25/61; ☺May–mid-Nov; P❄@🗘) Located 2 miles from downtown on the Maryland side of the Potomac River, this friendly hostel has plenty of amenities, including a kitchen, laundry and lounge area with games and books.

Jackson Rose B&B $$
(☎304-535-1528; www.thejacksonrose.com; 1167 W Washington St; r Mon-Fri/Sat & Sun $135/150; ❄🗘) This marvelous 18th-century brick residence with stately gardens has three attractive guest rooms, including a room where Stonewall Jackson lodged briefly

during the Civil War. Antique furnishings and vintage curios are sprinkled about the house, and the cooked breakfast is excellent. It's a 600m walk downhill to the historic district. No children under 12.

Town's Inn INN $$
(☎304-932-0677; www.thetownsinn.com; 179 High St; r $120-140; ❄) Spread between two neighboring pre–Civil War residences, the Town's Inn has rooms ranging from small and minimalist to charming heritage-style quarters. It's set in the middle of the historic district and has an indoor-outdoor restaurant as well.

🍴 Eating

Potomac Grille AMERICAN $
(186 High St; mains $10-16; ☺noon-9pm) Serves good pub food (fish and chips, crab cakes, huge burgers) and local brews in an old-fashioned tavern atmosphere in the historic district. The outdoor patio has fine views over the train station and Maryland Heights.

Beans in the Belfry AMERICAN $
(☎301-834-7178; 122 W Potomac St, Brunswick, MD; sandwiches around $7; ☺9am-9pm Mon-Sat, 8am-7pm Sun; 🗘♿) Across the river in Brunswick, MD (roughly 10 miles east), you'll find this converted red-brick church sheltering mismatched couches and kitsch-laden walls, featuring light fare (chili, sandwiches, quiche) and a tiny stage where live folk, blues and bluegrass bands strike up several nights a week. Sunday jazz brunch ($18) is a hit.

Canal House AMERICAN $$
(1226 Washington St; mains $11-24; ☺noon-8pm Mon, to 9pm Fri & Sat, to 6pm Sun; ♿) Roughly 1 mile west (and uphill) from the historic district, Canal House is a perennial favorite for delicious sandwiches, locally sourced seasonal fare and friendly service in a flower-trimmed stone house. Outdoor seating. You can bring your own beer or wine.

Anvil AMERICAN $$
(☎304-535-2582; www.anvilrestaurant.com; 1270 Washington St; lunch mains $8-12, dinner mains $20-28; ☺11am-9pm Wed-Sun) High-end mountain cuisine of the fresh field-and-stream variety is done up in any number of mouthwatering ways here. If crab, country ham and a pleasantly rural dining setting doesn't get you to the door, what will?

MARKVANDYKEPHOTOGRAPHY/GETTY IMAGES ©

Harpers Ferry National Historic Park (p79)

South Carolina

Moss-draped oaks. Stately mansions. Wide beaches. Rolling mountains. And an ornery streak as old as the state itself. Ah yes, South Carolina, where the accents are thicker and the traditions more dear.

From its Revolutionary War patriots to its 1860s secessionist government to its current crop of outspoken legislators, the Palmetto State has never shied away from a fight.

From the silvery sands of the Atlantic Coast, the state climbs westward from the Coastal Plain across the Piedmont and up into the Blue Ridge Mountains. Most travelers stick to the coast, with its splendid antebellum cities and palm-tree-studded beaches. But the interior has a wealth of sleepy old towns, wild and undeveloped state parks and spooky black-water swamps. Along the sea islands you hear the sweet songs of the Gullah, a culture and language created by former slaves who held onto many West African traditions through the ravages of time.

ℹ Information

South Carolina Department of Parks, Recreation & Tourism (☑ 803-734-1700; www.discoversouthcarolina.com; 1205 Pendleton St, Columbia; 🛜) Sends out the state's official vacation guide. The state's nine highway welcome centers offer free wi-fi. Ask inside for password.

South Carolina State Parks (☑ camping reservations 866-345-7275, 803-734-0156; www.southcarolinaparks.com) The helpful website lists activities and hiking trails, and allows online reservations for campsites ($6 to $40 per night).

Charleston

This lovely city will embrace you with the warmth and hospitality of an old and dear friend – who died in the 18th century. We jest, but the cannons, cemeteries and carriage rides do conjure an earlier era. And that historical romanticism, along with the food and Southern graciousness, is what makes Charleston one of the most popular tourist destinations in the South, drawing more than 4.8 million visitors every year.

How best to enjoy its charms? Charleston is a city for savoring – stroll past the historic buildings, admire the antebellum architecture, stop to smell the blooming jasmine and enjoy long dinners on the verandah. It's also a place for romance; everywhere you turn another blushing bride is standing on the steps of yet another charming church.

In the high season the scent of gardenia and honeysuckle mixes with the tang of horses from the aforementioned carriage tours that clip-clop down the cobblestones. In winter the weather is milder and the crowds thinner, making Charleston a great bet for off-season travel.

⊙ Sights

⊙ Historic District

The quarter south of Beaufain and Hasell Sts has the bulk of the antebellum mansions, shops, bars and cafes. At the southernmost tip of the peninsula are the antebellum mansions of the Battery. A loose path, the Gateway Walk, winds through several church grounds and graveyards between St John's Lutheran Church (5 Clifford St) and St Philip's Church (146 Church St).

Old Exchange & Provost Dungeon HISTORIC BUILDING
(www.oldexchange.org; 122 E Bay St; adult/child 7-12yr $10/5; ⊙9am-5pm; 🚻) Kids love the creepy dungeon, used as a prison for pirates and for American patriots held by the British during the Revolutionary War. The cramped space sits beneath a stately Georgian-Palladian custom house completed in 1771. Costumed guides lead the dungeon tours. Exhibits about the city are displayed on the upper floors.

Combination ticket with the Old Slave Mart Museum is adult/child $15/8.

Old Slave Mart Museum MUSEUM
(www.nps.gov/nr/travel/charleston/osm.htm; 6 Chalmers St; adult/child 5-17yr $7/5; ⊙9am-5pm Mon-Sat) Ryan's Mart was an open-air market that auctioned African men, women and children in the mid-1800s. It's now a museum about South Carolina's shameful past. Exhibits give insight into the slave experience; leg shackles and other artifacts are especially chilling. First-hand stories can be heard through the oral recollections of former slave Elijah Green and others.

A combination ticket with the Old Exchange is adult/child $15/8.

Gibbes Museum of Art GALLERY
(www.gibbesmuseum.org; 135 Meeting St; adult/child $9/7; ⊙10am-5pm Tue-Sat, 1-5pm Sun) Houses a decent collection of American and Southern works. The contemporary collection includes works by local artists, with Lowcountry life as a highlight. The museum was closed for renovations in 2015 but is scheduled to reopen in the spring of 2016.

Battery & White Point Gardens GARDENS
The Battery is the southern tip of the Charleston Peninsula, buffered by a seawall. Stroll past cannons and statues of military heroes in the gardens then walk the promenade and look for Fort Sumter.

Kahal Kadosh Beth Elohim SYNAGOGUE
(www.kkbe.org; 90 Hasell St; ⊙tours 10am-noon & 1:30-3:30pm Mon-Thu, 10am-noon & 1-3pm Fri, 1-3:30pm Sun) The oldest continuously used

synagogue in the country. There are free docent-led tours; check website for times.

Rainbow Row AREA
With its candy-colored houses, this stretch of lower E Bay St is one of the most photographed areas of town. The houses are around the corner from White Point Garden.

Historic Homes

About half a dozen majestic historic homes are open to visitors. Discounted combination tickets may tempt you to see more, but one or two will be enough for most people. Guided tours run every half-hour and start before the closing times noted in our reviews.

Aiken-Rhett House HISTORIC BUILDING
(www.historiccharleston.org; 48 Elizabeth St; adult/child 6-16yr $12/5; ⊙10am-5pm Mon-Sat, 2-5pm Sun) The only surviving urban plantation, this house gives a fascinating glimpse into antebellum life. The role of slaves is also presented, and you can wander into their dorm-style quarters behind the main house. The Historic Charleston Foundation manages the house with a goal of preserving and conserving, but not restoring, the property, meaning there have been few alterations.

Joseph Manigault House   HISTORIC BUILDING
(www.charlestonmuseum.org; 350 Meeting St; adult/child 13-17yr/child 3-12yr $12/10/5; ☻9am-5pm Mon-Sat, noon-5pm Sun) The three-story Federal-style house was once the showpiece of a French Huguenot rice planter. Don't miss the tiny neoclassical temple in the garden.

Nathaniel Russell House   HISTORIC BUILDING
(www.historiccharleston.org; 51 Meeting St; adult/child 6-16yr $12/5; ☻10am-5pm Mon-Sat, 2-5pm Sun) A spectacular, self-supporting spiral staircase is the highlight at this 1808 Federal-style house, built by a Rhode Islander, known in Charleston as 'the king of the Yankees.' The small but lush English garden is also notable, as is the square-circle-rectangle footprint of the home.

☻ Marion Square

Formerly home to the state weapons arsenal, this 10-acre park is Charleston's living room, with various monuments and an excellent Saturday farmers market.

Charleston Museum   MUSEUM
(www.charlestonmuseum.org; 360 Meeting St; adult/child 13-17yr/child 3-12yr $12/10/5; ☻9am-5pm Mon-Sat, noon-5pm Sun) Founded in 1773, this claims to be the country's oldest museum. It's helpful and informative if you're looking for historical background before strolling through the historic district. Exhibits spotlight various periods of Charleston's long and storied history.

Artifacts include a whale skeleton, slave tags and the 'secession table' used for the signing of the state's secession documents. And don't miss Charleston's polar bear.

☻ Aquarium Wharf

Aquarium Wharf surrounds pretty Liberty Sq. It's a great place to stroll and watch the tugboats guiding ships into the fourth-largest container port in the US. The wharf is one of two embarkation points for tours to Fort Sumter; the other is at Patriot's Point.

Fort Sumter   HISTORIC SITE
The first shots of the Civil War rang out at Fort Sumter, on a pentagon-shaped island in the harbor. A Confederate stronghold, the fort was shelled to bits by Union forces from 1863 to 1865. A few original guns and fortifications give a feel for the momentous history. The only way to get here is by boat tour (✆boat tour 843-722-2628, park 843-

883-3123; www.nps.gov/fosu; adult/child 4-11yr $19/12), which depart from 340 Concord St at 9:30am, noon and 2:30pm in summer (less frequently in winter) and from Patriot's Point in Mt Pleasant, across the river, at 10:45am, 1:30pm and 4pm from mid-March to late August (less frequently the rest of the year).

☞ Tours

Listing all of Charleston's walking, horse-drawn carriage, bus and boat tours could take up this entire book. Ask at the visitor center for the gamut.

Culinary Tours of Charleston   CULINARY
(✆843-722-8687; www.culinarytoursofcharleston.com; 2½hr tour $50) You'll likely sample grits, pralines and BBQ on the Savor the Flavors of Charleston walking tour of restaurants and markets.

Adventure Harbor Tours   BOAT
(✆843-442-9455; www.adventureharbortours.com; adult/child 3-12yr $55/30) Runs fun trips to uninhabited Morris Island – great for shelling.

Charleston Footprints   WALKING
(✆843-478-4718; www.charlestonfootprints.com; 2hr tour $20) A highly rated walking tour of historical Charleston sights.

⚑ Festivals & Events

Lowcountry Oyster Festival   FOOD
(www.charlestonrestaurantassociation.com/low-country-oyster-festival; ☻Jan) Oyster-lovers in Mt Pleasant feast on 80,000lb of the salty bivalves in January.

Spoleto USA   PERFORMING ARTS
(www.spoletousa.org; ☻May) This 17-day performing-arts festival is Charleston's biggest event, with operas, dramas and concerts staged across the city.

MOJA Arts Festival   PERFORMING ARTS
(www.mojafestival.com; ☻Sep) Spirited poetry readings and gospel concerts mark this two-week celebration of African American and Caribbean culture.

⌂ Sleeping

Staying in the historic downtown is the most attractive option, but it's also the most expensive, especially on weekends and in high season. The rates below are for high season (spring and early summer). The chain hotels on the highways and near the airport offer significantly lower rates. Hotel parking in central downtown is usually between $12 and $20 a night; accommodations on the fringes of downtown often have free parking.

The city is bursting with charming B&Bs serving Southern breakfasts and Southern hospitality. They fill up fast, so try using an agency such as **Historic Charleston B&B** (☑ 843-722-6606; www.historiccharlestonbedand breakfast.com; 57 Broad St; ☺ 9am-5pm Mon-Fri).

James Island County Park CAMPGROUND $
(☑ 843-795-4386; www.ccprc.com; 871 Riverland Dr; tent sites from $25, 8-person cottages $169; ☎) A great budget option, this 643-acre park southwest of downtown has meadows, a marsh and a dog park. Rent bikes and kayaks or play the disc golf course. The park offers shuttle services to downtown and Folly Beach ($10). Reservations are highly recommended. There are 124 campsites and 10 marsh-adjacent rental cottages. Cottages require a one-week rental June to August.

1837 Bed & Breakfast B&B $$
(☑ 877-723-1837, 843-723-7166; www.1837bb.com; 126 Wentworth St; r $135-189; P ✳ ☎) Close to the College of Charleston, this B&B may bring to mind the home of your eccentric, antique-loving aunt. The 1837 has nine charmingly overdecorated rooms, including three in the old brick carriage house.

Indigo Inn BOUTIQUE HOTEL $$
(☑ 843-577-5900; www.indigoinn.com; 1 Maiden Lane; r $249; P ✳ ☎ ☳) Our favorite part? The tasty ham biscuits at breakfast. Other perks include a prime location in the middle of the historic district and an oasis-like private courtyard, where guests can enjoy free wine and cheese by the fountain. Decor gives a nod to the 18th century, and the beds are quite comfy. Pets are $40 per night.

Town & Country Inn & Suites HOTEL $$
(☑ 843-571-1000; www.thetownandcountryinn. com; 2008 Savannah Hwy; r/ste from $169/189; P ✳ @ ☎ ☳) About 6 miles from downtown, Town & Country offers modern and stylish rooms at a reasonable price. The inn is a good launchpad if you want to get a jump on traffic for a morning visit to the Ashley River plantations.

★**Ansonborough Inn** HOTEL $$$
(☑ 800-522-2073; www.ansonboroughinn.com; 21 Hasell St; r from $299; P ✳ @ ☎) Droll neo-Victorian touches like the Persian-carpeted glass elevator, the closet-sized British pub and the formal portraits of dogs add a sense

Fort Sumter
GABRIELLE HOVEY/SHUTTERSTOCK ©

of fun to this intimate historic district hotel, which also manages to feel like an antique sailing ship. Huge guest rooms mix old and new, with worn leather couches, high ceilings and flat-screen TVs.

Complimentary wine and cheese social, with great pimiento cheese, runs from 5pm to 6pm.

Vendue Inn INN $$$
(☑ 843-577-7970; www.vendueinn.com; 19 Vendue Range; r/ste $265/435; P ✳ ☎) Fresh off a $4.8 million revamp and expansion, this boutique inn exudes a smart modern style that is also very inviting. Reimagined as an art hotel, it displays artwork property-wide, and the inn itself unfurls like a masterpiece of architecture and design. Simplicity and comfort blend seamlessly in rooms in the main building, while eye-catching art adds oomph to classically styled rooms across the street.

The popular Rooftop Bar is worth a stop even if you're not staying here. Parking is $16 per night.

✗ Eating

Charleston is one of America's finest eating cities, and there are enough fabulous restaurants here for a town three times its size. The 'classic' Charleston establishments stick to fancy seafood with a French flair, while many of the trendy up-and-comers are reinventing Southern cuisine with a focus on the area's copious local bounty, from oysters

UNDERSTANDING THE WAR

The Civil War began in April 1861, when the Confederacy attacked Fort Sumter in Charleston, SC, and it raged on for the next four years. By the end, more than 600,000 soldiers were dead; Southern plantations and cities lay sacked and burned. The North's industrial might provided an advantage, but its victory was not preordained; it unfolded, battle by bloody battle.

As fighting progressed, Abraham Lincoln recognized that if the war didn't end slavery outright, victory would be pointless. In 1863 his Emancipation Proclamation expanded the war's aims and freed all slaves. In April 1865, Confederate General Robert E Lee surrendered to Union General Ulysses S Grant in Appomattox, VA. The Union had been preserved, but at a staggering cost.

to heirloom rice to heritage pork. On Saturday, stop by the terrific **farmers market** (Marion Sq; ☺8am-1pm Sat Apr-Oct).

Sugar Bakeshop　　　　　　BAKERY $
(www.sugarbake.com; 59 1/2 Cannon St; pastries under $4; ☺10am-6pm Mon-Fri, 11am-5pm Sat) The staff is as sweet as the cupcakes at Sugar, a teensy space north of downtown. If available, try the Lady Baltimore cupcake, a retro Southern specialty with dried fruit and white frosting.

Artisan Meat Share　　　SANDWICHES $
(www.artisanmeatsharecharleston.com; 33 Spring St; sandwiches $7-12; ☺11am-7pm Mon-Fri, 10am-7pm Sat & Sun) Meat, man, meat. Stuffed in a biscuit. Piled high on potato bread. Or lurching across your charcuterie board – damn that's fresh. Order at the counter, find a seat if you can, then give a nod to artisan hipsters, bless their hearts. You know the drill: fresh, local, delicious and the condiments are housemade. The pea and peanut salad is superb.

Gaulart & Maliclet　　　　FRENCH $
(www.fastandfrenchcharleston.com; 98 Broad St; breakfast under $7, lunch $5-9, dinner $5-18; ☺8am-4pm Mon, to 10pm Tue-Thu, to 10:30pm Fri & Sat) Oooh la la. Locals crowd around the shared tables at this tiny spot, known as 'Fast & French,' to nibble on Gallic cheeses and sausages or nightly specials ($16) that include bread, soup, a main dish and wine.

Fleet Landing　　　　　　SEAFOOD $$
(☑843-722-8100; www.fleetlanding.net; 186 Concord St; lunch $9-23, dinner $10-26; ☺11am-4pm daily, 5-10pm Sun-Thu, to 11pm Fri & Sat) Come here for the perfect Charleston lunch: a river view, a cup of she-crab soup with a splash of sherry, and a big bowl of shrimp and grits. Housed in an old naval building on a pier, Fleet Landing is a convenient and scenic spot to enjoy fresh fish, a fried seafood platter or a burger after a morning of downtown exploring.

Smothered in tasso ham gravy, the shrimp and grits here look dirty, not high-falutin', and they're our favorite version in the city.

Poe's Tavern　　　　　PUB FOOD $$
(www.poestavern.com; 2210 Middle St, Sullivan's Island; mains $9-13; ☺11am-2am) On a sunny day the front porch of Poe's, on Sullivan's Island, is the place to be. The tavern's namesake, master of the macabre Edgar Allan Poe, was once stationed at nearby Fort Moultrie. The burgers are superb, and the Amontillado comes with guacamole, jalapeño jack, pico de gallo and chipotle sour cream. Quoth the raven: 'Gimme more.'

Xiao Bao Biscuit　　　　ASIAN $$
(www.xiaobaobiscuit.com; 224 Rutledge Ave, cnr of Spring St; lunch $10, dinner small plates $8-10, mains $12-17; ☺11:30am-2pm & 5:30-10pm Mon-Sat) Exposed brick walls, concrete floor and housed in a former gas station – this casual but stylish eatery hits the hipster high marks. But the food? Now we're talking. The short but palate-kicking menu spotlights simple pan-Asian fare enhanced by local ingredients and spicy flavors. For something different and memorable, try the *okonomiyaki* – a cabbage pancake – with egg and bacon.

Hominy Grill　　　　NEW SOUTHERN $$
(www.hominygrill.com; 207 Rutledge Ave; breakfast $8-16, lunch & dinner mains $9-19; ☺7:30am-9pm Mon-Fri, 9am-9pm Sat, to 3pm Sun; ☑) Slightly off the beaten path, this neighborhood cafe serves modern, vegetarian-friendly Lowcountry cuisine in an old barbershop. The shaded patio is tops for brunch.

★**FIG**　　　　　　　NEW SOUTHERN $$$
(☑843-805-5900; www.eatatfig.com; 232 Meeting St; mains $29-31; ☺5:30-10:30pm Mon-Thu, to 11pm Fri & Sat) FIG has been a long-time foodie favorite, and it's easy to see why. Welcoming staff, efficient but unrushed service, and top-notch nouvelle Southern fare from

James Beard Award–winner Mike Lata. The six nightly dishes embrace what's fresh and local from the sea and local farms and mills. FIG stands for Food is Good. And the gourmands agree.

Reservations highly recommended, but rogue solos might be able to snag a seat quickly at the communal table or bar.

Drinking & Nightlife

Balmy Charleston evenings are perfect for lifting a cool cocktail or dancing to live blues. Check out the weekly *Charleston City Paper* and the 'Preview' section of Friday's *Post & Courier*.

Husk Bar   BAR
(www.huskrestaurant.com; 76 Queen St; ⊙ from 4pm) Adjacent to Husk restaurant, this intimate brick-and-worn-wood spot recalls a speakeasy, with historic cocktails such as the Monkey Gland (gin, OJ, raspberry syrup).

Rooftop at Vendue Inn   BAR
(www.vendueinn.com; 23 Vendue Range; ⊙ 11:30am-10pm Sun-Thu, to midnight Fri & Sat) This rooftop bar has the best views of downtown, and the crowds to prove it. Enjoy craft beers, cocktails and live music on Sundays (6pm to 9pm).

Blind Tiger   PUB
(www.blindtigercharleston.com; 36-38 Broad St; ⊙ 11am-2am) A cozy and atmospheric dive, with stamped-tin ceilings, a worn wood bar and good pub grub.

Closed for Business   PUB
(www.closed4business.com; 453 King St; ⊙ 11am-2am Mon-Sat, 10am-2pm Sun) A wide beer selection and raucous neighborhood pub vibe.

Shopping

The historic district is clogged with overpriced souvenir shops and junk markets. Head instead to King St: hit lower King for antiques, middle King for cool boutiques, and upper King for trendy design and gift shops. The main stretch of Broad St is known as 'Gallery Row' for its many art galleries.

Shops of Historic
Charleston Foundation   GIFTS
(www.historiccharleston.org; 108 Meeting St; ⊙ 9am-6pm Mon-Sat, noon-5pm Sun) This place showcases jewelry, home furnishings and furniture inspired by the city's historic homes.

Charleston Crafts Cooperative   CRAFTS
(www.charlestoncrafts.org; 161 Church St; ⊙ 10am-6pm) A pricey, well-edited selection of contemporary South Carolina–made crafts such as sweetgrass baskets, hand-dyed silks and wood carvings.

Blue Bicycle Books   BOOKS
(www.bluebicyclebooks.com; 420 King St; ⊙ 10am-7:30pm Mon-Sat, 1-6pm Sun) Excellent new-and-used bookshop with a great selection on Southern history and culture.

ℹ Information

The City of Charleston maintains free public internet (wi-fi) access throughout the downtown area.

Charleston City Paper (www.charlestoncity paper.com) Published each Wednesday, this alt-weekly has good entertainment and restaurant listings.

Police Station (✐ nonemergencies 843-577-7434; 180 Lockwood Blvd) The police station is just northwest of downtown.

Post & Courier (www.postandcourier.com) Charleston's daily newspaper.

Post Office (www.usps.com; 83 Broad St; ⊙ 11:30am-3:30pm) At the corner of Broad and Meeting Sts.

University Hospital (Medical University of South Carolina; ✐ 843-792-1414; www.musc health.org; 171 Ashley Ave; ⊙ 24hr) Emergency room.

Visitor Center (✐ 843-853-8000; www. charlestoncvb.com; 375 Meeting St; ⊙ 8:30am-5:30pm Apr-Oct, to 5pm Nov-Mar) Find help with accommodations and tours or watch a half-hour video on Charleston history in this spacious renovated warehouse.

Patriot's Point Naval & Maritime Museum

Patriot's Point Naval & Maritime Museum (✐ 866-831-1720; www.patriotspoint. org; 40 Patriots Point Rd; adult/child 6-11yr $20/12; ⊙ 9am-6:30pm) is home to the USS *Yorktown*, a giant aircraft carrier used extensively in WWII. You can tour the ship's flight deck, bridge and ready rooms and get a glimpse of what life was like for its sailors. Also on-site is a submarine, a naval destroyer, the Medal of Honor Museum and a re-created 'fire base' from Vietnam. You can also catch the Fort Sumter boat tour (p84). Parking is $5.

Ashley River Plantations

Three spectacular plantations line the Ashley River about a 20-minute drive from downtown Charleston. You'll be hard-pressed for time to visit all three in one outing, but you could squeeze in two (allow at least a couple of hours for each). Ashley River Rd is also known as SC 61, which can be reached from downtown Charleston via Hwy 17.

⊙ Sights

★ Middleton Place HISTORIC BUILDING
See p29.

Drayton Hall HOUSE
See p28.

Magnolia Plantation HOUSE, GARDENS
(www.magnoliaplantation.com; 3550 Ashley River Rd; adult/child 6-10yr $15/10, tours $8; ⊙ 8am-5:30pm Mar-Oct, to 4:30pm Nov-Feb) Up for a spooky stroll? Then follow the boardwalk through the trees and bog on the Swamp Garden tour – it's a unique experience. The 500-acre plantation, which has been owned by the Drayton family since 1676, is a veritable theme park. Enjoy a tram tour, a petting zoo and a guided house tour. At the reconstructed slave cabins, the Slavery to Freedom Tour traces the African American experience at the plantation.

🛏 Sleeping

The Inn at Middleton Place INN $$
(☏ 843-556-0500; www.theinnatmiddletonplace. com; 4290 Ashley River Rd; r incl breakfast $180-400; ☎) In contrast to the antebellum plantation houses on Ashley River Rd, this cool inn is a series of eco-friendly modernist glass boxes overlooking the Ashley River. Rooms have shuttered floor-to-ceiling windows, handcrafted furniture and hardwood floors. Rate includes admission for two to the plantation.

Edisto Island

From just north of Charleston, the southern half of the South Carolina coast is a tangle of islands cut off from the mainland by inlets and tidal marshes. Here, descendants of West African slaves known as the Gullah maintain small communities in the face of resort and golf-course development. The landscape ranges from tidy stretches of shimmery, oyster-gray sand to wild, moss-shrouded maritime forests.

Edisto Island (ed-is-tow) is a homespun family vacation spot without a single traffic light. At its southern tip, **Edisto Beach State Park** (p32) has a gorgeous, uncrowded beach and oak-shaded hiking trails and campgrounds.

🍴 Eating

King's Farm Market FRESH PRODUCE $
(2559 Hwy 174, Edisto Island; ⊙ 9am-5pm Mon-Fri, to 4pm Sun, closed Jan) It's not just about the fresh produce, the macadamia nut cookies, the key lime pie, the blackberry cobbler, the breakfast quiche, or the sandwiches and casseroles. It's also about the easy-going friendliness. C'mon already, come in.

Beaufort & Hilton Head

The southernmost stretch of South Carolina's coast is popular with a mostly upscale set of golfers and B&B aficionados, but the area's got quirky charms aplenty for everyone.

On Port Royal Island the darling colonial town of **Beaufort** (byoo-furt) is often used as a set for Hollywood films about the South. The streets of the historic district are lined with antebellum homes and magnolias dripping with Spanish moss. The riverfront downtown has gobs of linger-worthy cafes and galleries.

South of Beaufort, some 20,000 young men and women go through boot camp each year at the **Marine Corps Recruit Depot** on Parris Island, made notorious by Stanley Kubrick's *Full Metal Jacket*. The facility has been 'welcoming' recruits for 100 years. Come for Friday graduations to see newly minted marines parade proudly for family and friends. You may be asked to show ID and car registration before entry to the base.

East of Beaufort, the Sea Island Pkwy/Hwy 21 connects a series of marshy, rural islands, including **St Helena Island**, considered the heart of Gullah country and the site of a coastal state park.

Across Port Royal Sound, tiny **Hilton Head Island** is South Carolina's largest barrier island and one of America's top golf spots. There are dozens of courses, many enclosed in posh private residential communities called 'plantations.' The overall setup is a bit unwelcoming. Summer traffic and miles of stoplights also make it hard to appreciate the beauty of the island, but there are some lush nature preserves and wide, white beaches hard enough for bike riding. Stop by the **visitor center** (📞800-523-3373; www.hiltonheadisland.org; 1 Chamber of Commerce Dr; ⊙8:30am-5:30pm Mon-Fri), on the island, for information and brochures.

Sights

Parris Island Museum   MUSEUM
(📞843-228-2951; www.mcrdpi.marines.mil; 111 Panama St; ⊙10am-4:30pm) **FREE** This fascinating museum has antique uniforms and weaponry, and covers marine corps history. There are also a few rooms dedicated to local history. Don't miss the introductory movie.

Penn Center   MUSEUM
(📞843-838-2474; www.penncenter.com/museum; 16 Penn Center Circle W; adult/child 6-16yr $5/3; ⊙9am-4pm Mon-Sat) Once the home of one of the nation's first schools for freed slaves, the Penn Center on St Helena Island has a small museum that covers Gullah culture and traces the history of Penn School.

Hunting Island State Park   PARK
(📞843-838-2011; www.southcarolinaparks.com; 2555 Sea Island Pkwy; adult/child 6-15yr $5/3; ⊙visitor center 9am-5pm Mon-Fri, 11am-5pm Sat & Sun) Lush and inviting, Hunting Island State Park impresses visitors with acres of spooky maritime forest, tidal lagoons and an empty, bone-white beach. The Vietnam War scenes from *Forrest Gump* were filmed in the marsh, a nature-lover's dream. Campgrounds fill up quickly in summer. Climb the **lighthouse** (admission $2; ⊙10am-4:45pm Mar-Oct) for sweeping coastal views.

Sleeping & Eating

Hunting Island State Park Campground   CAMPGROUND $
(📞reservations 866-345-7275, office 843-838-2011; www.southcarolinaparks.com; 2555 Sea Island Pkwy; tent sites $18.50-29, RV sites $23-32, cabin $210; ⊙6am-6pm, to 9pm early Mar-early Nov) At South Carolina's most visited park, you can camp under pine trees or palm trees. Several campsites are just steps from the beach. All sites are available by walk-up or reservation, but reservations are advisable in summer.

City Loft Hotel   HOTEL $$
(📞843-379-5638; www.citylofthotel.com; 301 Carteret St, Beaufort; r/ste $209/229; 🛜🎿) The

chic City Loft Hotel adds a refreshing dash of modern style to a town heavy on historic homes and stately oak trees. Enjoy flat-screen TVs in the bedroom and bathroom, artisan-tile showers and Memory Foam–topped beds. Other perks include a gym, complimentary bicycle use and an on-site coffee shop.

Cuthbert House   B&B $$$
(📞843-521-1315; www.cuthberthouseinn.com; 1203 Bay St; r incl breakfast $185-250; 🅿🎿🛜) The most romantic of Beaufort's B&B's, this sumptuously grand white-columned mansion is straight out of *Gone with the Wind II*. Antique furnishings are found throughout, but monochromatic walls add a fresh, modern feel. Some rooms have a river view. On his march through the South in 1865, General William T Sherman slept at the house.

Sgt White's   SOUTHERN, BARBECUE $
(1908 Boundary St, Beaufort; meat & three platters $9; ⊙11am-3pm Mon-Fri) A retired Marine sergeant serves up classic meat and three platters. At the counter, order your juicy BBQ ribs or meat dish, then choose three sides, which can include collards, okra stew and cornbread.

STRETCH
YOUR LEGS
CHARLESTON

Start/Finish: Husk

Distance: 1.8 miles

Duration: Three to four hours

Few cities evoke the same storied romanticism as Charleston. But the romance can overshadow the darker elements of the city's past. This stroll, which includes a slave mart, a dungeon and a city park, examines the city's compelling but contradictory history.

Take this walk on Trip

Husk

Every great walking tour begins with just the right lunch, which is always a sure thing at Husk (☎ 843-577-2500; www.huskrestaurant.com; 76 Queen St; brunch & lunch $10-16, dinner $27-30; ☒ 11:30am-2:30pm Mon-Sat, 5:30-10pm Sun-Thu, 5:30-11pm Fri & Sat, brunch 10am-2:30pm Sun). The creation of acclaimed chef Sean Brock, Husk is one the South's most buzzed-about restaurants. Everything on the menu is grown or raised in the South, and the menu changes daily. The setting, in a two-story mansion, is elegant but unfussy.

The Walk ≫ Follow Queen St east to Meeting St. Turn right. Walk one block south to Chalmers St, the city's red-light district in the 1700s. Cross Church St. The museum is ahead on the left.

Old Slave Mart

Charleston was a major marketplace for the African slave trade. In 1856 the city banned the selling of slaves on the streets, which drove merchants indoors. The Old Slave Mart Museum (p83) sits inside one of the resulting auction houses. Text-heavy exhibits illuminate the slave experience and slave trading; the few artifacts, such as leg shackles, are especially chilling. For first-hand stories, listen to the oral recollections of former slave Elijah Green, born in 1853.

Save $2 with a combination ticket to the Old Exchange.

The Walk ≫ Continue east on Chalmers St to State St and turn right. Walk south to Broad St. Turn left. The Old Exchange is one block ahead.

Old Exchange & Provost Dungeon

This 1771 Georgian-Palladian custom house (p83) is certainly impressive, but it's the brick dungeon underneath that wows the crowds. On the docent-led tour of this basement space, you'll learn about the pirates imprisoned here in 1718 when it was part of a battery guard house. The British kept American patriots captive in the space during the Revolutionary War. After the war, several of them returned to the building to ratify the United States Constitution.

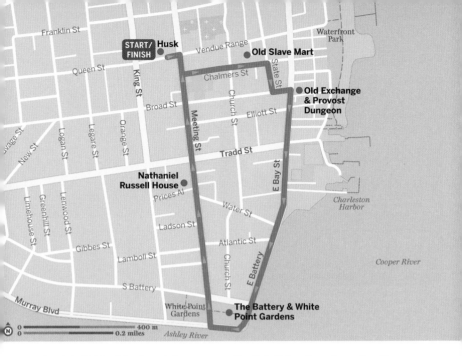

The Walk >> Follow E Bay St south. As you climb onto the promenade, grab your camera for photos of Rainbow Row, a line-up of candy-colored townhouses.

The Battery & White Point Gardens

Soak in more history at the Battery, the southern tip of the Charleston Peninsula, which is buffered by a seawall. Fortifications and artillery were placed here during the Civil War. In the gardens, stroll past cannons and statues of military heroes, and ponder the risk-filled lives of the pirates who were hanged here. From the promenade, look for Fort Sumter. The island fortress was fired upon by Confederates on April 12, 1861 – the first shots of the Civil War.

The Walk >> From the gardens, walk north on Meeting St.

Nathaniel Russell House

Built in 1808, the Federal-style Nathaniel Russell House (p84) is noted especially for its spectacular, self-supporting spiral staircase and its English garden. Russell, a merchant from Rhode Island, was known in Charleston as 'the king of the Yankees'. The home underwent major renovations in 2013, which added exhibits and preserved architectural features.

The Walk >> Continue north on Meeting St. Its junction with Broad St is known as the Four Corners of the Law, with a post office, a state courthouse, City Hall and a church each occupying one of the corners. Broad St here is known as Gallery Row. Follow Meeting St to Queen St for a cocktail at the speakeasy-style bar at Husk.

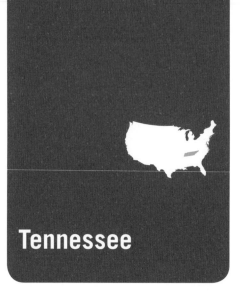

Tennessee

Most states have one official state song. Tennessee has seven. And that's not just a random fact – Tennessee has music deep within its soul.

Here in Tennessee, the folk music of the Scots-Irish in the eastern mountains combined with the bluesy rhythms of the African Americans in the western Delta to give birth to the modern country music that makes Nashville famous.

These three geographic regions, represented by the three stars on the Tennessee flag, have their own unique beauty: the heather-colored peaks of the Great Smoky Mountains; the lush green valleys of the central plateau around Nashville; and the hot, sultry lowlands near Memphis.

In Tennessee you can hike shady mountain trails in the morning, and by evening whoop it up in a Nashville honky-tonk or walk the streets of Memphis with Elvis' ghost.

❶ Information

Department of Environment & Conservation (☎ 888-867-2757; www.state.tn.us/environment/parks) Check out the well-organized website for camping, hiking and fishing info for Tennessee's more than 50 state parks.

Department of Tourist Development (☎ 615-741-2159; www.tnvacation.com; 312 8th Ave N, Nashville) Has welcome centers at the state borders.

Memphis

Memphis doesn't just attract tourists. It draws pilgrims. Music-lovers lose themselves to the throb of blues guitar on Beale St. Barbecue connoisseurs descend to stuff themselves silly on smoky pulled pork and dry-rubbed ribs. Elvis fanatics fly in to worship at the altar of the King at Graceland. You could spend days hopping from one museum or historic site to another, stopping only for barbecue, and leave happy.

But once you get away from the lights and the tourist buses, Memphis is a different place entirely. Named after the capital of ancient Egypt, it has a certain baroque ruined quality that's both sad and beguiling. Though poverty is rampant – Victorian mansions sit beside tumbledown shotgun shacks (a narrow style of house popular in the South) and college campuses lie in the shadow of eerie abandoned factories – whiffs of a renaissance are in the air.

Neighborhoods once downtrodden, abandoned and/or otherwise reclaimed by kudzu – South Main, Binghampton, Crosstown and others – are being reinvented with kitschy boutiques, hipster lofts and daring restaurants, all dripping with Memphis' wild river-town spirit.

The former Lorraine Motel, site of Martin Luther King Jr's assassination in 1968

◉ Sights

◉ Downtown

The pedestrian-only stretch of Beale St is a 24-hour carnival zone, where you'll find deep-fried funnel cakes, to-go beer counters, and music, music, music. Although locals don't hang out here much, visitors tend to get a kick out of it. Look out for the Memphis Music Hall of Fame and the Blues Hall of Fame, both of which opened in 2015.

★National Civil Rights Museum   MUSEUM
(Map p96; www.civilrightsmuseum.org; 450 Mulberry St; adult/child $15/12, student & senior $14; ⊙9am-5pm Mon & Wed-Sat, 1-5pm Sun Sep-May, to 6pm Jun-Aug) Housed across the street from the Lorraine Motel, where the Rev Dr Martin Luther King Jr was fatally shot on April 4, 1968, is the gut-wrenching National Civil Rights Museum. Five blocks south of Beale St, this museum's extensive exhibits and detailed timeline chronicle the struggle for African American freedom and equality. Both Dr King's cultural contribution and his assassination serve as prisms for looking at the Civil Rights movement, its precursors and its continuing impact on American life.

The turquoise exterior of the 1950s motel and two preserved interior rooms remain much as they were at the time of King's death.

Memphis Rock 'n' Soul Museum   MUSEUM
(Map p96; www.memphisrocknsoul.org; 191 Beale St; adult/child $12/9; ⊙10am-7pm) The Smithsonian's museum, next to FedEx Forum, examines how African American and white music mingled in the Mississippi Delta to create the modern rock and soul sound.

Gibson Beale Street
Showcase   FACTORY TOUR
See p37.

WC Handy House Museum   MUSEUM
(Map p96; www.wchandymemphis.org; 352 Beale St; adult/child $6/4; ⊙11am-4pm Tue-Sat winter, to 5pm summer) On the corner of 4th St, this shotgun shack once belonged to the composer called the 'father of the blues.' He was the first to transpose the 12-bar blues and later wrote 'Beale Street Blues' in 1916.

Peabody Ducks   MARCHING DUCKS
(Map p96; www.peabodymemphis.com; 149 Union Ave; ⊙11am & 5pm; 🚹) FREE A tradition dating to the 1930s begins every day at 11am sharp when five ducks file from the Peabody Hotel's gilded elevator, waddle across the red-carpeted lobby, and decamp in the marble lobby fountain for a day of happy splashing. The ducks make the reverse march at 5pm, when they retire to their penthouse accompanied by their red-coated Duckmaster.

Get here early to secure your spot among the heavy crowds (the mezzanine has the best views).

◉ North of Downtown

Mud Island   PARK
(Map p96; www.mudisland.com; 125 N Front St; ⊙10am-5pm Tue-Sun mid-Apr–Oct; ♠) **FREE**
A small peninsula jutting into the Mississippi, Mud Island is downtown Memphis' best-loved green space. Hop the monorail ($4, or free with Mississippi River Museum admission) or walk across the bridge to the park, where you can jog and rent bikes.

Slave Haven Underground Railroad Museum/Burkle Estate   MUSEUM
(www.slavehavenundergroundrailroadmuseum.org; 826 N 2nd St; adult/child $10/8; ⊙10am-4pm Mon-Sat, to 5pm Jun-Aug) This unimposing clapboard house is thought to have been a way station for runaway slaves on the Underground Railroad, complete with trapdoors, cellar entry and cubbyholes.

◉ East of Downtown

★ **Sun Studio**   STUDIO TOUR
(☑800-441-6249; www.sunstudio.com; 706 Union Ave; adult/child $12/free; ⊙10am-6:15pm, tours hourly 10:30am-5:30pm, no children under 5yr, Graceland shuttle hourly from 11:15am) This dusty storefront is ground zero for American rock and roll music. Starting in the early 1950s, Sun's Sam Phillips recorded blues artists such as Howlin' Wolf, BB King and Ike Turner, followed by the rockabilly dynasty of Jerry Lee Lewis, Johnny Cash, Roy Orbison and, of course, the King himself (who started here in 1953).

◉ Overton Park

Stately homes surround this 342-acre rolling green oasis – home to the Memphis Zoo – off Poplar Ave in the middle of this often gritty city. If Beale St is Memphis' heart, then Overton Park is its lungs.

Brooks Museum of Art   GALLERY
(www.brooksmuseum.org; 1934 Poplar Ave; adult/child $7/3; ⊙10am-4pm Wed & Fri, to 8pm Thu, to 5pm Sat, from 11am Sun) At this well-regarded art museum on the park's western fringe, the excellent permanent collection encompasses everything from Renaissance sculpture to Impressionist and abstract expressionist artworks.

Levitt Shell   ARCHITECTURE, CONCERT VENUE
(www.levittshell.org; 1928 Poplar Ave) A historic band shell and the site of Elvis' first concert in 1954. Today the mod-looking white shell hosts free concerts all summer.

◉ South of Downtown

★ **Graceland**   HISTORIC BUILDING
(☑901-332-3322; www.graceland.com; Elvis Presley Blvd/US 51; tours house only adult/child $36/16, expanded tours from $40/19; ⊙9am-5pm Mon-Sat, to 4pm Sun, shorter hours & closed Tue Dec; P) If you only make one stop in Memphis, it should be here: the sublimely kitschy, gloriously bizarre home of the King of Rock and Roll. Born in Mississippi, Elvis Presley was raised in the public housing projects of Memphis, inspired by blues clubs on Beale St, and discovered at Sun Studio. In the spring of 1957, the famous 22-year-old spent $100,000 on a mansion named Graceland.

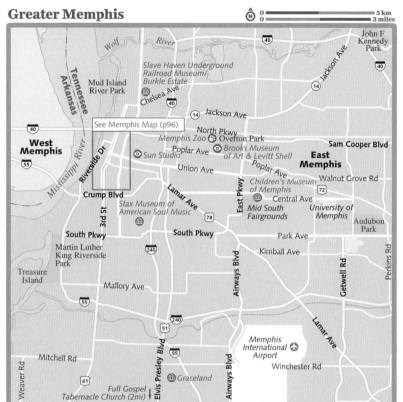

The King himself had the place, ahem, redecorated in 1974. With a 15ft couch, fake waterfall, yellow vinyl walls and green shag-carpet ceiling – it's a virtual textbook of ostentatious '70s style. You'll begin your tour at the visitor plaza on the other side of Elvis Presley Blvd. Book ahead in the busy season (June to August and important Elvis dates) to ensure a prompt tour time. The basic self-guided mansion tour comes with an engaging multimedia iPad narration. Pay just $4 extra to see the car museum, and $9 extra to tack on the two custom planes (check out the blue-and-gold private bathroom on the *Lisa Marie*, a Convair 880 Jet).

In 1982 Priscilla Presley (who divorced Elvis in 1973) opened Graceland to tours, and now millions come to pay homage to the King who died here (in the upstairs bathroom) from heart failure in 1977. Throngs of fans still weep at his grave, next to the swim-ming pool out back. Graceland is 9 miles south of downtown on US 51, also called 'Elvis Presley Blvd.' A free shuttle runs from Sun Studio (p94). Parking costs $10.

★ **Stax Museum of
American Soul Music** MUSEUM
(📞 901-942-7685; www.staxmuseum.com; 926 E McLemore Ave; adult/child $13/10; ⊙10am-5pm Tue-Sat, 1-5pm Sun) Wanna get funky? Head directly to Soulsville USA, where this 17,000-sq-ft museum sits on the site of the old Stax recording studio. This venerable spot was soul music's epicenter in the 1960s, when Otis Redding, Booker T and the MGs and Wilson Pickett recorded here.

Dive into soul-music history with photos, displays of '60s and '70s stage clothing and, above all, Isaac Hayes' 1972 Superfly Cadillac outfitted with shag-fur and 24-carat-gold exterior trim.

Memphis

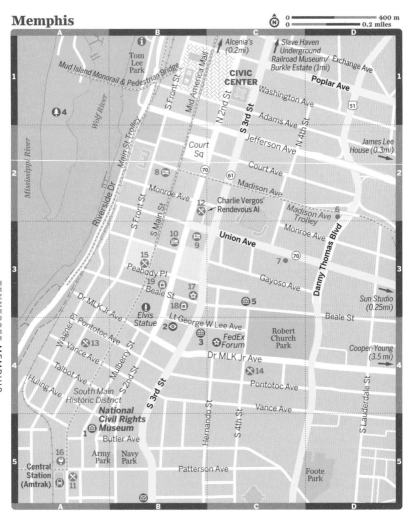

N 0 ——————— 400 m
0 ——————— 0.2 miles

Map labels (Memphis):

Mud Island Monorail & Pedestrian Bridge · Tom Lee Park · Mud Island Monorail & Pedestrian Bridge · Pedestrian Bridge · Mid America Mall · Alcenia's (0.2mi) · Slave Haven Underground Railroad Museum/ Burkle Estate (1mi) · Exchange Ave · CIVIC CENTER · Poplar Ave · Washington Ave · Wolf River · Mississippi River · Riverside Dr · Main St Trolley · S Front St · N 2nd St · S 3rd St · N 4th St · Adams Ave · Jefferson Ave · 51 · James Lee House (0.3mi) · Court Sq · Court Ave · 70 · 61 · Madison Ave · Monroe Ave · S Front St · S Main St · Charlie Vergos' Rendevous Al · Madison Ave Trolley · Monroe Ave Trolley · Union Ave · Danny Thomas Blvd · Peabody Pl · Beale St · Gayoso Ave · 70 · Sun Studio (0.25mi) · Dr MLK Jr Ave · Dr A Pontotoc Ave · Elvis Statue · Lt George W Lee Ave · Beale St · Robert Church Park · Cooper-Young (3.5 mi) · Wagner Pl · Vance Ave · Mulberry St · S 2nd St · S 3rd St · FedEx Forum · Dr MLK Jr Ave · Pontotoc Ave · Hernando St · S 4th St · Vance Ave · S Lauderdale St · Talbot Ave · Huling Ave · South Main Historic District · National Civil Rights Museum · Butler Ave · Army Park · Navy Park · Patterson Ave · Foote Park · Central Station (Amtrak)

✨ Festivals & Events

Trolley Night ART
(www.gosouthmain.com/trolley-night.html; S Main St; ⊙ 6-9pm last Fri of month) FREE On Trolley Night galleries on South Main stay open late and pour wine for the people.

Beale Street Music Festival MUSIC
See p40.

🛏 Sleeping

Chain motels lie off I-40, exit 279, across the river in West Memphis, AR. Look out for a new Guest House at Graceland, a 450-room luxury hotel steps from Graceland.

🛏 Downtown

Talbot Heirs GUESTHOUSE **$$**
(Map p96; ☎ 901-527-9772; www.talbothouse.com; 99 S 2nd St; ste $130-195; ✳ @ 🛜) Inconspicuously located on the 2nd floor of a busy downtown street, this cheerful guesthouse is

Memphis

one of Memphis' best kept and most unique secrets. Spacious suites are more like hip studio apartments than hotel rooms, with Asian rugs, funky local artwork and kitchens stocked with (included!) snacks.

Big stars like Harvey Keitel, Matt Damon and John Grisham, have nested here as well as Bobby Whitlock of Derek and the Dominos fame, who signed a piano.

Peabody Hotel HOTEL $$
(Map p96; ☏901-529-4000; www.peabodymem phis.com; 149 Union Ave; r from $219; ❄ 🛜 🏊) Memphis' most storied hotel has been catering to a who's who of Southern gentry since the 1860s. The current incarnation, a 13-story Italian Renaissance Revival–style building, dates to the 1920s and remains a social center, with a spa, shops, restaurants, an atmospheric lobby bar and 464 guest rooms in soothing turquoise tones.

Madison Hotel BOUTIQUE HOTEL $$$
(Map p96; ☏901-333-1200; www.madisonhotel memphis.com; 79 Madison Ave; r from $259; 🅿❄@🛜🏊) If you're looking for a sleek treat, check into these swanky, music-themed boutique sleeps. The rooftop Sky Terrace ($10 for nonguests) is one of the best places in town to watch a sunset, and stylish rooms have nice touches like hardwood entryways, high ceilings and Italian linens.

★ James Lee House B&B $$$
(☏901-359-6750; www.jamesleehouse.com; 690 Adams Ave; r $245-450; 🅿❄@🛜) This exquisite Victorian mansion sat abandoned for 56 years in the city's historic Victorian Village on the edge of downtown; $2 million later and

the owner's keen eye for detail and design has created one of Memphis' most refined sleeps.

Dating in parts to 1848 and 1872, a glorious renovation preserved crown moldings, mirrors, cornices, 14 fireplaces and some hardwood flooring. The five spacious suites are impeccably furnished, and there's a peaceful garden with original fountain.

🛏 South of Downtown

Graceland RV Park & Campground CAMPGROUND $
(☏901-396-7125; www.graceland.com/visit/ graceland_campground.aspx; 3691 Elvis Presley Blvd; tent sites/cabins from $25/47; 🅿🛜🏊) Keep Lisa Marie in business when you camp out or sleep in the no-frills log cabins (with shared bathrooms) next to Graceland.

Heartbreak Hotel HOTEL $$
(☏901-332-1000; www.graceland.com/visit/heart breakhotel.aspx; 3677 Elvis Presley Blvd; d from $115; 🅿❄@🛜🏊) At the end of Lonely St (seriously) across from Graceland, this basic hotel is tarted up with all things Elvis. Ramp up the already-palpable kitsch with one of the themed suites, such as the red-velvet Burnin' Love room. Good value.

Days Inn Graceland MOTEL $$
(☏901-346-5500; www.daysinn.com; 3839 Elvis Presley Blvd; r from $100; 🅿❄🛜🏊) With a guitar-shaped pool, gold records and Elvis memorabilia in the lobby and neon Cadillacs on the roof, the Days Inn manages to out-Elvis the neighboring Heartbreak Hotel. Guest rooms themselves are clean but nothing special.

Neon signs, Memphis
WALTER BIBIKOW/GETTY IMAGES ©

Eating

Downtown

**Gus's World Famous
Fried Chicken**   FRIED CHICKEN $
(Map p96; 310 S Front St; plates $5.65-9.95;
⊙11am-9pm Sun-Thu, to 10pm Fri & Sat)
Fried-chicken connoisseurs across the globe
twitch in their sleep at night, dreaming
about the gossamer-light fried chicken at
this downtown concrete bunker with the
fun, neon-lit interior and vintage jukebox.
On busy nights, waits can top an hour.

LUNCHBOXeats   SOUTHERN $
(Map p96; www.lunchboxeats.com; 288 S 4th St;
sandwiches $8-11; ⊙10:30am-3pm; 🐾) Classic
soul food gets a seriously tasty makeover
at this creative sandwich shop, resulting in
such ridiculousness as chicken and waffle
sandwiches (Belgian waffles serve as the
slices of 'bread'); crawfish étoufée sloppy
joes; a pork butt, onion and mac 'n' cheese
club sandwich and more, all served on traditional school lunch trays.

Alcenia's   SOUTHERN $
(www.alcenias.com; 317 N Main St; mains $9.55-
11; ⊙11am-5pm Tue-Fri, 9am-3pm Sat) The only
thing sweeter than Alcenia's famous 'Ghetto-
Aid' (a diabetes-inducing fruit drink) is
owner Betty-Joyce 'BJ' Chester-Tamayo –

don't be surprised to receive a kiss on the
top of the head as soon as you sit down.

The lunch menu at this funky little gold-
and-purple-painted cafe rotates daily – look
for killer fried chicken and catfish, melt-in-
the-mouth spiced cabbage and an exquisite
eggy custard pie.

Arcade   DINER $
(Map p96; www.arcaderestaurant.com; 540 S Main
St; mains $7-10; ⊙7am-3pm Sun-Wed, to 11pm Thu-
Sat) Step inside this ultra-retro diner, Memphis' oldest, and wander to the Elvis booth,
strategically located near the rear exit. The
King used to sit here and eat griddle-fried
peanut butter and banana sandwiches and
would bolt out the door if fan-instigated
pandemonium ensued. Crowds still pack
in for sublime sweet-potato pancakes – as
fluffy, buttery and addictive as advertised.
The rest of the dishes are standard greasy-
spoon fare (don't tell Elvis).

Charlie Vergos' Rendezvous   BARBECUE $$
(Map p96; ☏901-523-2746; www.hogsfly.com; 52
S 2nd St; mains $8-20; ⊙4:30-10:30pm Tue-Thu,
11am-11pm Fri, from 11:30am Sat) Tucked in its
own namesake alleyway off Monroe Ave,
this subterranean institution sells an aston-
ishing 5 tons of its exquisite dry-rubbed ribs
weekly. The ribs don't come with any sauce,
but the pork shoulder does, so try a com-
bo and you'll have plenty of sauce to enjoy.
The beef brisket is also tremendous. Expect
a wait.

Majestic Grille   EUROPEAN $$$
(Map p96; ☏901-522-8555; www.majesticgrille.
com; 145 S Main St; mains $16-47; ⊙11am-10pm
Mon-Thu, to 11pm Fri & Sat, to 9pm Sun; 🐾) Set
in an old silent-movie theater near Beale St,
with pretalkie black and whites strobing in
the handsome dark-wood dining room, the
Majestic serves classic continental fare, from
roasted half chicken, to seared tuna and
grilled pork tenderloin, and four varieties of
hand-cut filet mignon.

East of Downtown

★ Payne's Bar-B-Q   BARBECUE $
(1762 Lamar Ave; sandwiches $4.50-8.50, plates
$7.50-10.50; ⊙11am-5:30pm Tue-Sat) We'd
say this converted gas station has the best
chopped-pork sandwich in town, but we
don't want to have to fight anyone.

Bar DKDC
GASTROPUB **$**

(www.bardkdc.com; 964 S Cooper St; dishes $5-14; ☺5pm-3am Tue-Sat) Cheap and flavorful global street food is the calling at this ever-evolving Cooper-Young staple. South American arepas, Vietnamese *banh mi* sandwiches, Caribbean jerked fish, Greek souvlaki – you get the idea. The space sports an eclectic decor, a chalkboard wine list and friendly bartenders.

Hog & Hominy
SOUTHERN, ITALIAN **$$**

(📞901-207-7396; www.hogandhominy.com; 707 W Brookhaven Circle; pizza $14-17; ☺11am-2pm & 5-10pm Tue-Thu, to late Fri-Sat, 10:30am-10pm Sun; 🐾) The chef-driven, Southern-rooted Italian at this Brookhaven Circle hot spot has grabbed the nation's attention, winning best-new-this and best-new-that from everyone from *GQ* to *Food & Wine* magazines. Small plates (often with adventurous ingredients like frog legs, pig ears and beef hearts) and perfect brick-oven pizza are the mainstays; along with seasonal cocktails, craft beers and bocce.

⭐ Restaurant Iris
NEW SOUTHERN **$$$**

(📞901-590-2828; www.restaurantiris.com; 2146 Monroe Ave; mains $27-39; ☺5-10pm Mon-Sat) Chef Kelly English crafts special, avant-garde Southern fusion dishes that delight foodies, hence the James Beard noms. He's got a fried-oyster-stuffed steak, a sublime shrimp and grits, and some scrumptious brussels sprouts dressed up with smoky bacon and sherry, all served in a refined residential home. Next door he has opened Second Line, a more affordable New Orleans bistro.

🍸 Drinking & Nightlife

The East Memphis neighborhoods of Cooper-Young and Overton Square offer the best concentration of hip bars and restaurants. Both are about 4 miles east of downtown. Last call is 3am.

⭐ Wiseacre Brewing Co
MICROBREWERY

(www.wiseacrebrew.com; 2783 Broad Ave; beers $5, tours $10; ☺4-9pm Wed-Fri, 1-9pm Sat) Our favorite Memphis taproom is in the warehouse district of Binghampton, 5 miles east of downtown. Sample year-round and seasonal craft brews on the outside deck, which features a wraparound porch hugging two enormous, near 100-year-old cement wheat silos.

Earnestine & Hazel's
BAR

(Map p96; www.earnestineandhazelsjukejoint.com; 531 S Main St; ☺5pm-3am Sun-Fri, from 11am Sat) One of the great dive bars in Memphis has a 2nd floor full of rusty bedsprings and claw-foot tubs, remnants of its brothel past. Its Soul Burger is the stuff of legend. Things heat up after midnight.

Hammer & Ale
BEER HALL

(www.hammerandale.com; 921 S Cooper; beers $5; ☺2-9pm Tue-Thu, 11am-10pm Fri-Sat, noon-3pm Sun; 🐾) Hopheads descend on this barn-like Cooper-Young craft beer bar decked out in light cypress woods throughout. Memphis breweries Wiseacre, High Cotton, Memphis Made and Ghost River are represented among the 24 taps of mostly Southern microbrews. Cash *not* accepted!

⭐ Entertainment

Beale St is the obvious spot for live blues, rock and jazz. There's no cover at most clubs, or it's only a few bucks, and the bars are open all day, while neighborhood clubs tend to start filling up around 10pm. Check the *Memphis Flyer* (www.memphisflyer.com) online calendar for listings.

Wild Bill's
BLUES

(1580 Vollintine Ave; cover Fri-Sat $10; ☺Wed-Thu noon-9pm, noon-3am Fri-Sat) Don't even think of showing up at this gritty hole-in-the-wall before midnight. Order a 40oz beer and a basket of wings then sit back to watch some of the greatest blues acts in Memphis from 11pm Friday and Saturday only. Expect some stares from the locals; it's worth it for the kick-ass, ultra-authentic jams.

Lafayette's Music Room
LIVE MUSIC

(📞901-207-5097; www.lafayettes.com/memphis; 2119 Madison Ave; cover Fri-Sat $5; ☺11am-10pm Mon-Wed, to midnight Tue & Sun, to 2am Fri-Sat) This newly reopened historic Overton Square music venue once hosted Kiss and Billy Joel in its '70s heyday. The lights were out for 38 years, but it's now one of the most intimate music venues in town.

Hi-Tone Cafe
LIVE MUSIC

(www.hitonememphis.com; 412-414 N Cleveland St; cover $5-20) In new digs in Crosstown, this unassuming little dive is one of the city's best places to hear live local bands and touring indie acts.

Young Avenue Deli   LIVE MUSIC
(www.youngavenuedeli.com; 2119 Young Ave; ⏰11am-3pm Mon-Sat, from 11:30am Sun) This Midtown favorite has food, pool, occasional live music and a young laid-back crowd.

Rum Boogie   BLUES
(Map p96; www.rumboogie.com; 182 Beale St) Huge, popular and loud, this Cajun-themed Beale St club hops every night to the tunes of a tight house blues band.

🛍 Shopping

Beale St abounds with cheesy souvenir shops, while Cooper-Young is the place for boutiques and bookshops. The streets around South Main have been branded an arts district.

City & State   FOOD & DRINK, ACCESSORIES
(www.cityandstate.us; 2625 Broad Ave; coffee $2.50-4.75; ⏰7am-6pm Mon-Sat, 8am-2pm Sun; 🛜) This fabulous new artisan-centric store and coffeehouse in Binghampton stocks exquisitely curated everyday coolness (hand-crafted soaps, boutique camping items, waxed canvas lunch bags, ceramic pour-over coffee mugs) and is the only place in Memphis for a barista-level coffee experience.

A Schwab's   GIFTS
(Map p96; www.a-schwab.com; 163 Beale St; ⏰noon-5pm Mon-Wed, to 6pm Thu, 10am-9pm Fri & Sat, 11am-5pm Sun) It has everything from denim shirts to flasks to rubber duckies to fine hats to overalls. But the real attractions are the antiques upstairs. Think vintage scales and irons, hat stretchers and a cast-iron anchor of a cash register.

Lanksy Brothers   CLOTHING
(Map p96; ☑901-425-3960; www.lanskybros.com; 126 Beale St; ⏰9am-6pm Sun-Wed, to 9pm Thu-Sat) The 'Clothier to the King,' this mid-century men's shop once outfitted Elvis with his two-tone shirts. Today it has a retro line of menswear (including blue suede shoes!) plus gifts and women's clothes.

ℹ Information

Commercial Appeal (www.commercialappeal.com) Daily newspaper with local entertainment listings.
Main Post Office (Map p96; www.usps.com; 555 S 3rd St; ⏰9:30am-6pm Mon-Fri) Downtown postal services.
Memphis Flyer (www.memphisflyer.com) Free weekly distributed on Wednesday; has entertainment listings.

Memphis Visitor's Center (☑888-633-9099; www.memphistravel.com; 3205 Elvis Presley Blvd; ⏰9am-6pm Apr-Sep, to 5pm Oct-Mar, to 4pm Sun Nov-Feb) City information center near the exit for Graceland.
Police Station (☑901-636-4099; www.memphispolice.org; 545 S Main St) Terribly hard to find. It's above Amtrak's Central Station.
Regional Medical Center at Memphis (☑901-545-7100; www.the-med.org; 877 Jefferson Ave) Has the only level-one trauma center in the region.
Tennessee State Visitor Center (☑901-543-6757; www.tnvacation.com; 119 N Riverside Dr; ⏰7am-11pm) Brochures for the whole state.

Shiloh National Military Park

'No soldier who took part in the two day Battle at Shiloh ever spoiled for a fight again,' said one veteran of the bloody 1862 clash, which took place among these lovely fields and forests. Ulysses S Grant led the Army of Tennessee. An intense Confederate assault on the first day took Grant by surprise. On the second day he responded with a creative maneuver that held Pittsburgh Landing and turned the Confederates back. During the fight over 3500 soldiers died and nearly 24,000 were wounded. A relative unknown at the beginning of the war, Grant went on to lead the Union to victory and eventually became the 18th president of the United States.

Vast **Shiloh National Military Park** (☑731-689-5696; www.nps.gov/shil; 1055 Pittsburg Landing Rd; ⏰park dawn-dusk, visitor center 8am-5pm) **FREE** is located just north of the Mississippi border near the town of Crump, TN, and can only be seen by car. Sights include the Shiloh National Cemetery, and an overlook of the Cumberland River at the landing site for Union reinforcement troops.

Nashville

Imagine you're an aspiring country singer arriving in downtown Nashville after days of hitchhiking, with nothing but your battered guitar on your back. Gaze up at the neon lights of Lower Broadway, take a deep breath of smoky, beer-perfumed air, feel the boot-stompin' rumble from deep inside the crowded honky-tonks, and say to yourself: 'I've made it.'

For country-music fans and wannabe songwriters all over the world, a trip to Nashville is the ultimate pilgrimage. Since the 1920s the city has been attracting musicians who have taken the country genre from the 'hillbilly music' of the early 20th century to the slick 'Nashville sound' of the 1960s to the punk-tinged alt-country of the 1990s.

Nashville's many musical attractions range from the Country Music Hall of Fame to the revered *Grand Ole Opry* to Jack White's niche of a record label. It also has a lively university community, some excellent down-home grub and some seriously kitschy souvenirs.

◉ Sights

◉ Downtown

The historic 2nd Ave N business area was the center of the cotton trade in the 1870s and 1880s, when most of the Victorian warehouses were built; note the cast-iron and masonry facades. Today it's the heart of the District, with shops, restaurants, underground saloons and nightclubs. It's a bit like the French Quarter meets Hollywood Boulevard drenched in bourbon and country twang. South of Lower Broadway is the SoBro district, revitalized by the opening of the $635-million Music City Center (www. nashvillemusiccitycenter.com; Broadway St, btwn 5th & 8th Aves), which houses a convention center, restaurants, bars and hotels. Two blocks west of 2nd Ave N, Printers Alley is a narrow cobblestoned lane known for its nightlife since the 1940s. Along the Cumberland River, Riverfront Park is a landscaped promenade that's being redeveloped; West Riverfront Park, an 11-acre civic park, will include over 1 mile of multiuse greenway trails, Nashville's first downtown dog park, ornamental gardens, a 1.5-acre event lawn called The Green and an amphitheater.

★ **Country Music
Hall of Fame & Museum**   MUSEUM
(www.countrymusichalloffame.org; 222 5th Ave S; adult/child $25/15, with audio tour $27/18, with Studio B 1hr tour $40/30; ⊙9am-5pm) Following a $100 million expansion in 2014, this monumental museum, reflecting the near-biblical importance of country music to Nashville's soul, is a must-see, whether you're a country music fan or not. Gaze at Carl Perkins' blue suede shoes, Elvis' gold Cadillac (actually white) and gold piano (actually gold), and Hank Williams' Western-cut suit with musical note appliqués.

Highlights of the ambitious 210,000-sq-ft expansion include the 800-seat CMA Theater, the Taylor Swift Education Center and the relocation of the legendary letterpress operation Hatch Show Print (p40). Written exhibits trace country's roots, computer touch screens access recordings and photos from the enormous archives, and the fact- and music-filled audio tour is narrated by contemporary stars.

Ryman Auditorium   HISTORIC BUILDING
(www.ryman.com; 116 5th Ave N; adult/child self-guided tours $15/10, backstage tours $20/15; ⊙9am-4pm) The so-called 'Mother Church of Country Music' has hosted a laundry list of performers, from Martha Graham to Elvis, and Katherine Hepburn to Bob Dylan. The soaring brick tabernacle (1892) was built by wealthy riverboat captain Thomas Ryman to house religious revivals, and watching a show from one of its 2000 seats can still be described as a spiritual experience.

The *Grand Ole Opry* (p41) took place here for 31 years until it moved out to the Opryland complex in Music Valley in 1974. Today the *Opry* returns to the Ryman during winter. In 2015 a $14 million visitor experience renovation installed a new event space, cafe and bars.

Johnny Cash Museum & Store   MUSEUM
(www.johnnycashmuseum.com; 119 3rd Ave; adult/child $16/12; ⊙8am-7pm) The new museum dedicated to 'The Man in Black' is smallish but houses the most comprehensive collection of Johnny Cash artifacts and memorabilia in the world, and is officially endorsed by the Cash family.

Tennessee State Museum
MUSEUM

(www.tnmuseum.org; 5th Ave, btwn Union & Deaderick Sts; 10am-5pm Tue-Sat, 1-5pm Sun;) **FREE** For history buffs, this engaging but not flashy museum on the ground floor of a massive office tower provides a worthy look at the state's past, with Native American handicrafts, a life-size log cabin and quirky historical artifacts such as President Andrew Jackson's inaugural hat.

Frist Center for the Visual Arts
GALLERY

(www.fristcenter.org; 919 Broadway; adult/child $12/free; 10am-5:30pm Mon-Wed & Sat, to 9pm Thu & Fri, 1-5pm Sun) A post office turned top-notch art museum and complex hosting traveling exhibitions of everything from American folk art to Picasso.

Tennessee State Capitol
HISTORIC BUILDING

(www.capitol.tn.gov; Charlotte Ave; tours 9am-4pm Mon-Fri) **FREE** This 1845–59 Greek Revival building was built from local limestone and marble by slaves and prison inmates working alongside European artisans. Around back, steep stairs lead down to the **Tennessee Bicentennial Mall**, whose outdoor walls are covered with historical facts about Tennessee's history, and the wonderful daily **Farmers Market**.

Free tours leave from the information desk on the 1st floor of the Capitol every hour on the hour.

West End

Along West End Ave, starting at 21st Ave, sits prestigious **Vanderbilt University**, founded in 1883 by railway magnate Cornelius Vanderbilt. The 330-acre campus buzzes with some 12,000 students, and student culture influences much of Midtown's vibe.

Parthenon
PARK, GALLERY

(www.parthenon.org; 2600 West End Ave; adult/child $6/4; 9am-4:30pm Tue-Sat, 12:30-4:30pm Sun) Yes, that is indeed a reproduction Athenian Parthenon sitting in **Centennial Park**. Originally built in 1897 for Tennessee's Centennial Exposition and rebuilt in 1930 due to popular demand, the full-scale plaster copy of the 438 BC original now houses an art museum with a collection of American paintings and a 42ft statue of the Greek goddess Athena.

Music Row
AREA

(Music Sq West & Music Sq East) Just west of downtown, sections of 16th and 17th Aves,

called Music Sq West and Music Sq East, are home to the production companies, record labels, agents, managers and promoters who run Nashville's country-music industry, including the famed RCA Studio B.

Music Valley

This suburban tourist zone is about 10 miles northeast of downtown at Hwy 155/Briley Pkwy, exits 11 and 12B, and reachable by bus.

Grand Ole Opry House
MUSEUM

(615-871-6779; www.opry.com; 2802 Opryland Dr; tours adult/child $22/17; tours 9am-4pm) This unassuming modern brick building seats 4400 for the *Grand Ole Opry* (p108) on Tuesdays, Fridays and Saturdays from March to November and Wednesdays from June to August. Guided backstage tours are offered every 15 minutes daily from October to March.

Willie Nelson Museum
MUSEUM

(www.willienelsongeneralstore.com; 2613 McGavock Pike; admission $8; 8:30am-9pm) 'Outlaw Country' star Willie Nelson sold all his worldly goods to pay off $16.7 million in tax debt in the early 1990s. You can see them at this quirky museum not far from the Grand Ole Opry House.

Outside Town

Hermitage
PLANTATION

(615-889-2941; www.thehermitage.com; 4580 Rachel's Lane; adult/child $20/14, with multimedia player $28/18; 8:30am-5pm mid-Mar–mid-Oct 15, 9am-4:30pm mid-Oct–mid-Mar) The former home of seventh president Andrew Jackson lies 15 miles east of downtown Nashville. The 1150-acre plantation is a peek into what life was like for a Mid-South gentleman farmer in the 19th century. Tour the Federal-style brick mansion, now a furnished house museum with costumed interpreters, and see Jackson's original 1804 log cabin and the old slave quarters (Jackson was a lifelong supporter of slavery, at times owning up to 100 slaves; a special exhibit tells their stories).

Belle Meade Plantation
PLANTATION

(615-356-0501; www.bellemeadeplantation.com; 5025 Harding Pike; adult/student 13-18yr/child under 13yr $18/12/10; 9am-5pm) The Harding-Jackson family began raising thoroughbreds here (6 miles west of Nashville) in the early 1800s. Several Kentucky Derby winners have been descendants of Belle Meade's studly sire, Bonnie Scotland, who died in 1880. Yes, Bonnie can be a boy's name! The 1853 mansion is open to visitors, as are various interesting outbuildings, including a model slave cabin. Wine tasting is available on-site, too.

★☆ Festivals & Events

CMA Music Festival MUSIC
(www.cmafest.com; ☉ Jun) Draws tens of thousands of country-music fans to town.

Tennessee State Fair FAIR
(www.tnstatefair.org; ☉ Sep) Nine days of racing pigs, mule-pulls and cake bake-offs.

⌨ Sleeping

Bargain-bin chain motels cluster on all sides of downtown, along I-40 and I-65. Music Valley has a glut of family-friendly midrange chains.

⌨ Downtown

★ Nashville Downtown Hostel HOSTEL **$**
(☑ 615-497-1208; www.nashvillehostel.com; 177 1st Ave N; dm $35-40, r $128-140; **P**) Well located and up-to-the-minute in style and function. The common space in the basement, with its rather regal exposed stone walls and beamed rafters, is your all-hours mingle den. Dorm rooms are on the 3rd and 4th floors, and have lovely wood floors, exposed timber columns, silver-beamed ceilings and four, six or eight bunks to a room.

Hotel Indigo BOUTIQUE HOTEL **$$**
(☑ 615-891-6000; www.hotelindigo.com; 301 Union St; r from $199; **P ☕ ✳ @ ☎**) Part of a boutique international chain, the Indigo has a fun, pop-art look, with 160 rooms (30 of which are brand new). Avoid the original (but tacky) Terrazo floor rooms in favor of those spacious King Rooms, with brand-new hardwood floors, high ceilings, flat-screens, leather headboards and office chairs.

Union Station Hotel HOTEL **$$$**
(☑ 615-726-1001; www.unionstationhotelnashville.com; 1001 Broadway; r from $259; **P ✳ ☎**) This soaring Romanesque gray stone castle was Nashville's train station back in the days when rail travel was a grand affair; today it's downtown's most iconic hotel. The vaulted lobby is dressed in peach and gold with inlaid marble floors and a stained-glass ceiling.

The Hermitage, Nashville

Rooms are tastefully modern, with flat-screen TVs and deep soaking tubs, and are set for an upcoming renovation.

Hermitage Hotel HOTEL **$$$**
(☑ 888-888-9414, 615-244-3121; www.thehermitagehotel.com; 231 6th Ave N; r from $399; **P ✳ ☎**) Nashville's first million-dollar hotel was a hit with the socialites when it opened in 1910. The beaux-arts lobby feels like a czar's palace, every surface covered in rich tapestries and ornate carvings. The original art-deco men's room, dating to the 1930s, is worth a pop-in, as is the Capitol Grille restaurant, which sources from its own farm.

Rooms are upscale, with plush, four-poster beds, marble baths with soaking tubs, and mahogany furniture (ask for those ending in -08-14 for Capitol views).

⌨ The Gulch

★ 404 BOUTIQUE HOTEL **$$$**
(☑ 615-242-7404; www.the404nashville.com; 404 12th Avenue S; r $275-425; **P ☕ ✳ @ ☎**) Guests let themselves in to Nashville's hippest – and smallest – hotel. Beyond the ebonized cedar frontage, industrial grays under violet lighting lead to five rooms in the minimalist space, most featuring painstakingly hip loft spaces. Local photography by Caroline Allison adds a splash of color. There's a restaurant in a shipping container, and local beers, sodas and parking are included.

Nashville

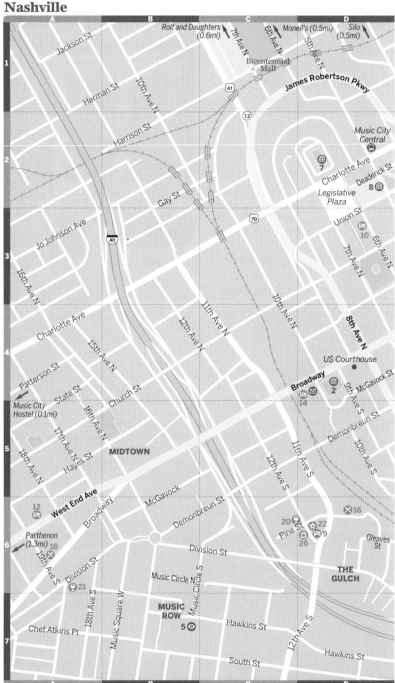

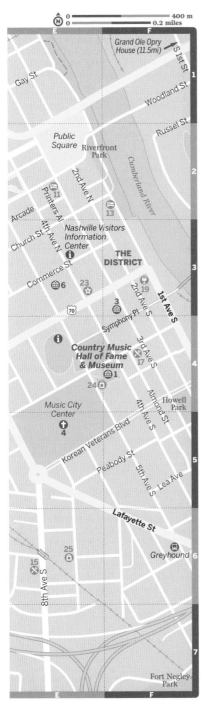

🛏 West End

Music City Hostel   HOSTEL **$**

(📞615-692-1277; www.musiccityhostel.com; 1809
Patterson St; dm $30-35, d $85-100; P❊@🛜)
These squat brick bungalows are less than
scenic, but Nashville's West End hostel is
lively and welcoming, with a common kitch-
en, outdoor grill and fire pit. The crowd is
young, international and fun, and many
hoppin' West End bars are within walking
distance.

Rooms are designed to function both as
dorms or privates, and some share showers
but have their own toilet.

Downtown Nashville
F11PHOTO/SHUTTERSTOCK ©

Hutton Hotel HOTEL $$$
(☏615-340-9333; www.huttonhotel.com; 1808 West End Ave; r from $259; P⊕☀@🛜) 🖉 One of our favorite Nashville boutique hotels riffs on midcentury-Modern design with bamboo-paneled walls and reclaimed WWI barn-wood flooring. Sizable rust- and chocolate-colored rooms are well appointed with electrically controlled marble rain showers, glass washbasins, king beds, ample desk space, wide flat-screen TVs and high-end carpet and linens. Sustainable luxury abounds. Take a free spin in the hotel's electric Tesla!

🛏 Music Valley

Gaylord Opryland Hotel RESORT $$
(☏866-972-6779, 615-889-1000; www.gaylord hotels.com; 2800 Opryland Dr; r from $199; P☀@🛜🏊) This whopping 2882-room hotel is a universe unto itself, the largest non-casino resort in the USA. Why set foot outdoors when you could ride a paddleboat along an artificial river, eat sushi beneath faux waterfalls in an indoor garden or sip Scotch in an antebellum-style mansion, all *inside* the hotel's three massive glass atriums.

✕ Eating

The classic Nashville meal is the 'meat-and-three' – a heaping portion of meat, served with your choice of three home-style sides. Gentrifying Germantown offers a hand-

ful of cafes and restaurants, including two standouts. Five Points in East Nashville is the epicenter of Nashville's hipster scene and is covered with cafes, restaurants and shops, with most of the action in the area of Woodlawn St between 10th and 11th.

✕ Downtown & Germantown

Arnold's SOUTHERN $
(www.arnoldscountrykitchen.com; 605 8th Ave S; meals $9-10; ⊙10:30am-2:45pm Mon-Fri) Grab a tray and line up with college students, garbage collectors and country-music stars at Arnold's, king of the meat-and-three. Slabs of drippy roast beef are the house specialty, along with fried green tomatoes, cornbread two ways, and big gooey wedges of chocolate meringue pie.

★ Rolf and Daughters MODERN EUROPEAN $$
(☏615-866-9897; www.rolfanddaughters.com; 700 Taylor St; mains $17-26; ⊙5:30-10pm; 🛜) The epicenter of Germantown's foodie revival is this stunning kitchen run by Belgian chef Philip Krajeck, whose earthy pastas, rustic sauces and seasonal 'modern peasant food' will stand your taste buds on end as if to say, 'What was *that*?'

Standouts of the European-inspired, locally sourced fare – it's a feeding frenzy here as the menu fluctuates with the arrival of the season's first crops – include *garganelli verde* (pasta that is green from fresh spinach) and a devastatingly good pastured chicken with preserved lemon and garlic confit. Reservations? Certainly. But there's a communal table and bar for walk-ins as well.

Silo NEW SOUTHERN $$
(☏615-750-2912; www.silotn.com; 1222 4th Ave N; mains $17-26; ⊙5-11pm Tue-Sun, bar from 4pm) This Southern-influenced farm-to-table bistro in Germantown is easy on the eyes: Amish-crafted carpentry and pendant lighting by artist John Beck. The food follows suit. Though the menu changes faster than your Twitter feed, dishes like braised rabbit in housemade pasta and pan-seared Gulf corvina pop with savory and rich deliciousness.

Monell's SOUTHERN $$
(☏615-248-4747; www.monellstn.com; 1235 6th Ave N; all you can eat $13-18; ⊙10:30am-2pm Mon, 8:30am-4pm & 5-8:30pm Tue-Fri, 8:30am-8:30pm Sat, 8:30am-4pm Sun) In an old brick house just north of the District, Monell's is beloved

for down-home Southern food served family style. This is not just a meal, it's an experience, as platter after platter of skillet-fried chicken, pulled pork, corn pudding, baked apples, mac and cheese and mashed potatoes keep coming...and coming. Clear your afternoon schedule!

★**Etch** MODERN AMERICAN **$$$**
(☑ 615-522-0685; www.etchrestaurant.com; 303 Demonbreun St; dinner mains $21-38; ⊙ 11am-2pm & 5-10pm Mon-Thu, 11am-2pm & 5-10:30pm Fri, 5-10:30pm Sat; ☎) Well-known Nashville chef Deb Paquette's Etch serves some of Nashville's most inventive cuisine – comfort food whose flavors and textures have been manipulated into tantalizing combinations that surpass expectations in every bite. Octopus and shrimp bruschetta, roasted cauliflower with truffled pea pesto, cocoa-chili-spiced venison, grilled filet with sourdough baked potato bread pudding – all masterpieces. Reservations essential.

✗ The Gulch

★**Biscuit Love** BREAKFAST **$**
(www.biscuitlovebrunch.com; 316 11th Ave; biscuits $10-14; ⊙ 7am-3pm; ☎) Championing everything that is wrong about American breakfasts, Biscuit Love started life as a food truck in 2012. Its gluttonous gourmet versions of the Southern biscuit-and-gravy experience took off, allowing it to graduate to this supremely cool brick-and-mortar location in the Gulch.

Look no further than the menu's first item, the East Nasty – a perfectly fluffy buttermilk biscuit smothered by an insanely good piece of fried chicken thigh, aged cheddar and perfect sausage gravy. If that's wrong, we don't wanna be right!

✗ West End & Midtown

★**Hattie B's** SOUTHERN **$**
(www.hattieb.com; 112 19th Ave S; quarter/half plates from $8.50/12; ⊙ 11am-10pm Mon-Thu, to midnight Fri-Sat, to 4pm Sun) Hattie's may be the hipsterized, social-media savvy yin to the traditional chicken shack's yang, but if this isn't Nashville's best cayenne-rubbed 'hot' fried chicken, our name is mud. Perfectly moist, high-quality bird comes devilishly fried to levels that top out at 'Shut the Cluck Up!' hot and they mean business ('Damn Hot' was our limit). Get in line.

✗ East Nashville

★**The Pharmacy** BURGERS, BEER GARDEN **$**
(www.thepharmacynashville.com; 731 Mcferrin Ave; burgers $8-11; ⊙ 11am-10pm Sun-Thu, to 11pm Fri-Sat; ☎) Prepare to go to war for a seat at this burger bar, constantly voted Nashville's best, be it at the welcoming communal table, bar or in the spectacular backyard beer garden. Tattooed staff sling burgers, sausages and old-school sides (tater tots!) washed back with specialty beers and hand-mixed old-fashioned sodas.

Pied Piper Creamery ICE CREAM **$**
(www.thepiedpipercreamery.com; 114 S 11th St; scoops $3.75; ⊙ noon-9pm Sun-Thu, to 10pm Fri & Sat) Thicker, smoother and more packed with goodness than any other ice-cream in town. How to choose: Toffee Loaded Coffee? Chocolate with Cinnamon and Cayenne Pepper? Trailer Trash, with Oreo, Reese's Pieces, Snickers, Butterfinger, Twix *and* Nestlé's Crunch? It's in Five Points.

🍷 Drinking & Nightlife

Nashville has the nightlife of a city three times its size, and you'll be hard-pressed to find a place that doesn't have live music. College students, bachelor-party-goers, Danish backpackers and conventioneers all rock out downtown, where neon-lit Broadway looks like a country-fried Las Vegas. Bars and venues in neighborhoods such as East Nashville, Hillsboro Village, Germantown, the Gulch, 12 South and SoBro tend to attract more locals, with many places clustered near Vanderbilt University.

★**Butchertown Hall** BEER HALL
(www.butchertownhall.com; 1416 Fourth Ave N; beer $5-8; ⊙ 11am-late Mon-Fri, from 10am Sat-Sun; ☎) This hipster hangout in Germantown plays to the neighborhood's historical roots. It's the first beer hall in the neighborhood since 1909. The 2200-sq-ft space is gorgeous: vaulted ceilings, oversized subway tiles, and stacked stone and chopped wood strategically used as earthy-accented space dividers. There are 31 taps specializing in local and rarer German options as well as cask-conditioned English ales.

The Latin-leaning, smoke-and-brimstone-heavy German-Southern comfort food is not to be missed, either.

Patterson House COCKTAIL BAR
(www.thepattersonnashville.com; 1711 Division St; cocktails $12-14; ⊙5pm-3am; 🛜) Without a doubt Nashville's best spot for artisanal cocktails, so much so there is often a wait (yes, for a drink at a bar!). There is no service without a seat, either at the 30-stool bar or in the surrounding banquets. Meticulous Prohibition-era mixology is sipped amid vintage chandeliers, and checks are delivered inside novels.

Acme Feed & Seed BAR, LIVE MUSIC
(www.theacmenashville.com; 101 Broadway; ⊙11am-late Mon-Fri, from 10am Sat-Sun; 🛜) This ambitious, four-floor takeover of an old 1875 farm-supply warehouse has finally given Nashvillians a reason to go downtown even when family is *not* visiting. The 1st floor is devoted to lightning-fast pub grub, craft beers and live music that's defiantly un-country most nights (Southern rock, indie, roots etc).

Head up a level for a casual cocktail lounge complete with rescued furniture, vintage pinball, walls made from old printing plates and a cornucopia of music memorabilia. And then there's the open-air rooftop, with unrivaled views over the Cumberland River and straight down the belly of Broadway.

Hops + Craft BAR
(www.hopscrafts.com; 319 12th Ave S; beer $4.75-6.60; ⊙2-11pm Mon-Thu, noon-midnight Fri, from 11am Sat, noon-11pm Sun; 🛜) You won't be raving about the ambience on any postcards home, but this small (and devoted!) bar in the Gulch is Nashville's best for diving head-first into the local craft beer scene. Knowledgeable and friendly bartenders offer tastings on any number of their 36 draft offerings.

★Barista Parlor COFFEE
(www.baristaparlor.com; 519 Gallatin Ave; coffee $5-6; ⊙7am-8pm Mon-Fri, 8am-8pm Sat-Sun) Unrepentantly hipster coffee joint housed inside a huge former transmission shop in East Nashville. Some of America's best beans are put through methods that all but fiendish coffee nerds will need defined (V60, Kone, Chemex etc). The lone turntable preserving vinyl is a mere afterthought. Prepare to wait – the art shall not be compromised.

The espresso comes courtesy of the famed, rare (and hand-built!) $18,000 Slayer machine.

☆ Entertainment

Nashville's opportunities for hearing live music are unparalleled. As well as the big venues, many talented country, folk, bluegrass, Southern-rock and blues performers play smoky honky-tonks, college bars, coffee shops and organic cafes for tips. Cover charges are rare.

★Station Inn LIVE MUSIC
(🖉615-255-3307; www.stationinn.com; 402 12th Ave S; ⊙open mike 7pm, live bands 9pm) Sit at one of the small cocktail tables, squeezed together on the worn wood floor in this beer-only dive, illuminated with stage lights and neon signs, and behold the lightning fingers of bluegrass savants. We are talking stand-up bass, banjo, mandolin, fiddle and a modicum of yodeling.

Famed duo Doyle and Debbie, a cult-hit parody of a washed-up country-music duo, perform most Tuesdays ($20; reservations essential on 🖉615-999-9244).

Bluebird Cafe CLUB
See p41.

Tootsie's Orchid Lounge HONKY-TONK
(🖉615-726-7937; www.tootsies.net; 422 Broadway; ⊙10am-late) FREE The most venerated of the downtown honky-tonks, Tootsie's is a blessed dive oozing boot-stomping, hillbilly, beer-soaked grace. In the 1960s club owner and den mother 'Tootsie' Bess nurtured Willie Nelson, Kris Kristofferson and Waylon Jennings on the come up. A new rooftop and stage, added in 2014, is one of Broadway's best parties-with-views.

Grand Ole Opry MUSICAL THEATER
(🖉615-871-6779; www.opry.com; 2802 Opryland Dr; tickets $40-70) Though you'll find a variety of country shows throughout the week, the performance to see is the *Grand Ole Opry,* a lavish tribute to classic Nashville country music, every Tuesday, Friday and Saturday night. Shows return to the Ryman (p101) from November to June.

🔒 Shopping

Lower Broadway has tons of record shops, boot stores and souvenir stalls. The 12th Ave South neighborhood is the spot for ultra-trendy boutiques and vintage stores.

★Hatch Show Print ART, SOUVENIRS
(www.hatchshowprint.com; 224 5th Ave S; tours $15; ⊙9:30am-5pm Mon-Fri) One of the oldest letterpress print shops in the US, Hatch has

been using old-school, hand-cut blocks to print its bright, iconic posters since vaudeville days. The company has produced graphic ads and posters for almost every country star since and have now graduated to newly expanded digs inside the revamped Country Music Hall of Fame (p101).

There are three daily tours (12:30pm, 2pm and 3:30pm); an expanded retail space; and a gallery, where you can purchase restrikes made from original wood plates dating from the 1870s to 1960s, and one-of-a-kind monoprints reinterpreted from original woodblocks by Nashville legend Jim Sherraden.

★**Third Man Records**   MUSIC
(www.thirdmanrecords.com; 623 7th Ave S; ⊙10am-6pm Mon-Sat, 1-4pm Sun) In a still-industrial slice of downtown you'll find Jack White's boutique record label, shop and novelty lounge, complete with its own lathe and live venue. It sells only Third Man recordings on vinyl and CD, collectible T-shirts, stickers, headphones and Pro-Ject record players. You'll also find White's entire catalog of recordings; and you can record yourself on vinyl ($15).

Live shows go off in the studio's Blue Room once a month. They're typically open to the public (about $10), but are only announced a couple weeks in advance. Attendees receive an exclusive colored vinyl Black and Blue of the performance.

Two Old Hippies   CLOTHING, LIVE MUSIC
(www.twooldhippies.com; 401 12th Ave S; ⊙10am-8pm Mon-Thu, to 9pm Fri-Sat, 11am-6pm Sun) Only in Nashville would an upscale retro-inspired clothing shop have a bandstand with regular live shows of high quality. And, yes, just like the threads, countrified hippie rock is the rule. The shop itself has special jewelry, fitted tees, excellent belts, made in Tennessee denim, a bounty of stage-worthy shirts and jackets, and some incredible acoustic guitars.

There's live music four nights a week at 6pm and an open mike for kids on Sundays at 1pm.

ⓘ Information

Main Police Station (☑615-862-7611; 601 Korean Veterans Blvd) Nashville's Central Precinct.

Nashville Scene (www.nashvillescene.com) Free alternative weekly with entertainment listings.

Nashville Visitors Information Center (☑800-657-6910, 615-259-4747; www.visitmusiccity.com; 501 Broadway, Bridgestone Arena; ⊙8am-5:30pm Mon-Sat, 10am-5pm Sun) Pick up free city maps here at the glass tower. A second, smaller center (150 4th Ave N; ⊙8am-5pm Mon-Fri) is run out of the corporate offices in the Regions Bank Building lobby.

Out & About Nashville (www.outandabout nashville.com) A monthly covering the local gay and lesbian scene.

Post Office (www.usps.com; 601 Broadway; ⊙6am-6pm Mon-Fri, to 12:30pm Sat) The most convenient downtown post office.

Tennessean (www.tennessean.com) Nashville's daily newspaper.

Vanderbilt University Medical Center (☑615-322-5000; www.mc.vanderbilt.edu; 1211 Medical Center Dr) Widely regarded as Tennessee's best hospital.

Franklin

About 20 miles south of Nashville off I-65, the historic town of Franklin (www.historic franklin.com) has a charming downtown and beautiful B&Bs. It was also the site of one of the Civil War's bloodiest battlefields. On November 30, 1864, 20,000 Confederates and 17,000 Union soldiers fought over a 2-mile stretch of Franklin's outskirts. Much of that battlefield has been turned into suburbs, but the Carter House (☑615-791-1861; www.boft.org; 1140 Columbia Ave, Franklin; adult/child $15/8; ⊙9am-5pm Mon-Sat, 11-5pm Sun; ⬇🅿) property preserves up to 20 acres of the Battle of Franklin. The house is one of the most bullet-ridden Civil War properties left in the USA.

STRETCH YOUR LEGS
NASHVILLE

Start/Finish: Country Music Hall of Fame & Museum

Distance: 2.7 miles

Duration: Three hours

Nashville will spin you around and leave your ears ringing with the sound of steel guitar. But it has a brainy side too, with great museums, and grand old government buildings not far from those addictive honky-tonks.

Take this walk on Trips

Country Music Hall of Fame & Museum

Head directly to downtown's Country Music Hall of Fame & Museum (www .countrymusichalloffame.com; 222 5th Ave S; adult/child $25/15, with audio tour $27/18, with Studio B 1hr tour $40/30; ☺9am-5pm). Here you can gawk at Patsy Cline's cocktail gown, Johnny Cash's guitar, Elvis' gold Cadillac and Conway Twitty's yearbook picture (back when he was Harold Jenkins). Exhibits trace country's roots from the original banjo-pickin' hillbillies of the early 20th century through to today's tattooed and pierced stars, while listening booths give you access to the vast archives of sound.

The Walk » Head north for one block on 5th Ave and make a right on Broadway.

The District

Lower Broadway between 2nd and 4th Aves is famous for its neon-lit honky-tonks, the crowds of tourists in painfully new cowboy boots, and the kid on the corner singing his heart out on a battered guitar. For rockabilly tunes, we love Robert's Western World (p40). Tootsie's Orchid Lounge (p108) is a classic beer-drenched joint, too. Both have free live music from 11am. And don't miss Hatch Show Print (p40), a long-running block-print company with a tremendous archive.

The Walk » Continue down Broadway until it dead ends at 1st Ave and the Cumberland River. Head upriver to Church St and make a left. Between Church and Union St you'll find Printer's Alley.

Printer's Alley

Cobblestone-paved Printer's Alley, now lined with bars and restaurants, used to be home to the city's thriving printing industry. Beginning in the early 1800s, horse carts carried paper and ink to the alley's mostly religious publishing houses. The printing of Christian hymnals gave way to secular music publishing, which helped attract the large record labels in the 1940s and '50s.

The Walk » Take Church to 5th Ave. Make a left and walk two long blocks to Nashville's most historical venue.

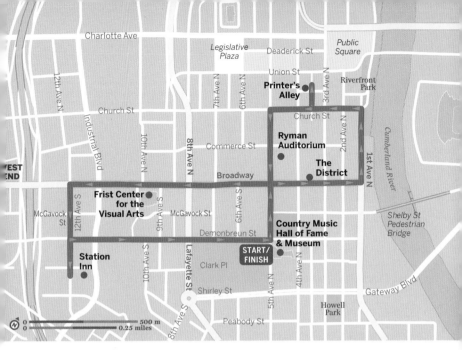

Ryman Auditorium

Ryman Auditorium (p101) is a soaring Gothic Revival building commissioned in the late 1800s by crusty old riverboat captain Thomas Ryman, after his soul was saved by a popular Christian evangelist. These days, the 2000-seat Ryman hosts distinctly secular acts such as alt-rock giants The National.

The Walk » Take 5th Ave to Broadway, make a right and walk for several blocks.

Frist Center for the Visual Arts

This massive art museum (p102) is on par with those you'll find in the world's great cities. It has a collection that spans indigenous American pottery to Picasso to mind-melting modernist sculpture;

contemporary works are installed on the 1st-floor gallery.

The Walk » Continue on Broadway to 12th Ave and make a left. In four blocks you'll find our favorite place in town for night music.

Station Inn

Station Inn (☎615-255-3307; www.stationinn.com; 402 12th Ave S; ☉open mike 7pm, live bands 9pm), an unassuming stone building, and beer-only dive, is the best place in town for serious bluegrass. We're talking stand-up bass, fiddle, banjo, mandolin and a bit of honey-throated yodeling. The room is lit only by stage lights, neon signs and the lightning fingers of bluegrass savants.

The Walk » Walk two blocks to Demonbreun St, which leads you back to the Hall of Fame.

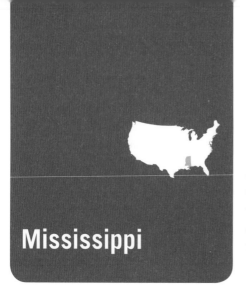

Mississippi

Oft mythologized and misunderstood, Mississippi is the womb of some of the rawest history – and music – in the country.

The state named for the most vital waterway in North America encompasses, appropriately enough, a long river of identities. Mississippi features palatial mansions and rural poverty; haunted cotton flats and lush hill country; honey-dipped sand on the coast and serene farmland in the north.

⊕ Getting There & Away

There are three routes most folks take when traveling through Mississippi. I-55 and US-61 both run north–south from the state's northern to southern borders. US-61 goes through the Delta, and I-55 flows in and out of Jackson. The gorgeous Natchez Trace Pkwy runs diagonally across the state from Tupelo to Natchez.

⊕ Information

Mississippi Division of Tourism Development (☑ 866-733-6477, 601-359-3297; www.visit mississippi.org) Has a directory of visitor bureaus and thematic travel itineraries. Most are well thought-out and run quite deep.

Mississippi Wildlife, Fisheries, & Parks (☑ 800-467-2757; www.mississippistateparks.reserve america.com) Camping costs from $13 (tent only) to $35 (beachfront camping), depending on the facilities; some parks have cabins for rent.

Oxford

Oxford both confirms and explodes preconceptions you may have of Mississippi's most famous college town. Frat boys in Ford pickup trucks and debutante sorority sisters? Sure. But they're alongside doctoral candidates debating critical theory, and a lively arts scene. Local culture revolves around the Square, where you'll find bars, restaurants and decent shopping, and the regal University of Mississippi (www.olemiss.edu).

⊙ Sights & Activities

The gorgeous, 0.6-mile-long and rather painless Bailee's Woods Trail connects two of the town's most popular sights: Rowan Oak and the University of Mississippi Museum. The Grove, the shady heart of Ole Miss (the university), is generally peaceful, except on football Saturdays, when it buzzes with one of the most unforgettable tailgating (pregame) parties in American university sports.

Rowan Oak   HISTORIC BUILDING
(☑ 662-234-3284; www.rowanoak.com; Old Taylor Rd; admission $5; ☺ 10am-4pm Tue-Sat, 1-4pm Sun, to 6pm Jun-Aug) Literary pilgrims head directly here, to the graceful 1840s home of William Faulkner. He authored many brilliant and dense novels set in Mississippi, and his work is celebrated in Oxford with an annual conference in July. Tours of Rowan Oak – where Faulkner lived from 1930 until his death in 1962, and which may reasonably be dubbed, to use the author's own elegant words, his 'postage stamp of native soil' – are self-guided.

University of Mississippi Museum MUSEUM
(www.museum.olemiss.edu; University Ave at 5th
St; admission $5; ⊙10am-6pm Tue-Sat) This
museum has fine and folk arts and a pleth-
ora of science-related exhibits, including
a microscope and electromagnet from the
19th century.

🛏 Sleeping & Eating

The cheapest accommodations are chains
on the outskirts of town. A number of
high-quality restaurants dot the Square.

5 Twelve B&B $$
(☑662-234-8043; www.the5twelve.com; 512 Van
Buren Ave; r $140-200, studio $200-250; 🅿✳🛜)
This six-room B&B has an antebellum-style
exterior and modern interior (think Tempur-
Pedic beds and flat-screen TVs). Room rates
include full Southern breakfast to order. It's
an easy walk from shops and restaurants,
and the hosts will make you feel like family.

Taylor Grocery SEAFOOD $$
(www.taylorgrocery.com; 4 County Rd 338A; dishes
$9-15; ⊙5-10pm Thu-Sat, to 9pm Sun) Be pre-
pared to wait – and to tailgate in the parking lot – at this splendidly rusticated catfish
haunt. Order fried or grilled (either way, it's
amazing) and bring a marker to sign your
name on the wall. It's about 7 miles from
downtown Oxford, south on Old Taylor Rd.

Ravine AMERICAN $$$
(☑662-234-4555; www.oxfordravine.com; 53 Coun-
ty Rd 321; mains $19-32; ⊙6-9pm Wed-Thu, to 10pm
Fri & Sat, 10:30am-2pm & 6-9pm Sun; 🛜) About 3
miles outside Oxford, this unpretentious, coz-
ily elegant restaurant nuzzles up to the forest.
Chef Joel Miller picks and pulls much of the
produce and herbs from his garden and buys
locally and organically whenever possible;
he's been doing it since before locavore was
a buzzword. The result is simply wonderful
food and a delicious experience.

City Grocery AMERICAN $$$
(☑662-232-8080; www.citygroceryonline.com;
152 Courthouse Sq; mains $26-32; ⊙11:30am-
2:30pm Mon-Sat, 6-10pm Mon-Wed, to 10:30pm
Thu-Sat, 11am-3pm Sun) Chef John Currance
won a James Beard Award and quickly
set about dominating the Oxford culinary
scene. City Grocery is one of his finest restaurants, offering a menu of haute Southern goodness like rice grits risotto and
lard-braised hanger steak. The upstairs bar,
decked out with local folk art, is a treat. Reservations recommended.

☆ Entertainment

On the last Tuesday of the month, an in-
creasingly popular Art Crawl connects galleries across town with free buses carrying
well-lubricated art lovers. Nibbles and wine
aplenty.

Proud Larry's LIVE MUSIC
(☑662-236-0050; www.proudlarrys.com; 211 S
Lamar Blvd; ⊙shows 9:30pm) On the Square,
this iconic music venue hosts consistently
good bands, and does a nice pub-grub business at lunch and dinner before the stage
lights dim.

The Lyric LIVE MUSIC
(☑662-234-5333; www.thelyricoxford.com; 1006
Van Buren St) This old brick house, now a
rather intimate theater with concrete floors,
exposed rafters and a mezzanine, is the place
to see indie rockers and folksy crooners.

🛍 Shopping

Square Books BOOKS
(☑662-236-2262; www.squarebooks.com; 160
Courthouse Sq; ⊙9am-9pm Mon-Thu, to 10pm
Fri & Sat, to 6pm Sun) Square Books, one of
the South's great independent bookstores,
is the epicenter of Oxford's lively literary
scene and a frequent stop for traveling authors. There's a cafe and balcony upstairs,
along with an immense section devoted to

Faulkner. Nearby Square Books Jr stocks children's and young-adult lit. Off Square Books (662-236-2828; 129 Courthouse Sq; 9am-9pm Mon-Sat, noon-5pm Sun) trades in used books.

Mississippi Delta

A long, low land of silent cotton fields bending under a severe sky, the Delta is a place of surreal, Gothic extremes. Here, in a feudal society of great manors and brutal enslavement, songs of labor and love became American pop music. It traveled via Africa to sharecropping fields along Hwy 61, unfolding into the blues, the father of rock and roll. Tourism in this area, which still suffers some of the worst rural poverty rates in the country, largely revolves around discovering the sweat-soaked roots of this original, American art form.

Clarksdale

Clarksdale is the Delta's most useful base. It's within a couple of hours of all the blues sights, and big-name blues acts are regular weekend visitors. But this is still a poor Delta town, and it's jarring to see how many businesses find private security details a necessity after dark.

◉ Sights

The Crossroads of Hwys 61 and 49 is supposedly the intersection where the great Robert Johnson made his mythical deal with the devil, immortalized in his tune 'Cross Road Blues.' Now all of the implied lonely fear and dark mysticism of the space is taken up by a tacky sculpture. For what it's worth, few historians agree where the actual crossroad is located.

Delta Blues Museum   MUSEUM
(662-627-6820; www.deltabluesmuseum.org; 1 Blues Alley; adult/senior & student $7/5; 9am-5pm Mon-Sat Mar-Oct, from 10am Nov-Feb) A small but well-presented collection of memorabilia is on display here. The shrine to Delta legend Muddy Waters includes the actual cabin where he grew up. Local art exhibits and a gift shop round out the display. Occasionally hosts live-music shows on Friday nights.

Rock & Blues Heritage Museum   MUSEUM
(901-605-8662; www.blues2rock.com; 113 E Second St; admission $5; 11am-5pm Tue-Sat)

A jovial Dutch transplant and blues fanatic has turned his immense personal collection of records, memorabilia and artifacts into a magic museum that traces the roots of blues and rock from the 1920s to the '70s.

★ Festivals & Events

Juke Joint Festival   MUSIC
(www.jukejointfestival.com; tickets $15; Apr) There are more than 120 venues at this three-day festival held in joints sprinkled in and around Clarksdale.

Sunflower River Blues
& Gospel Festival   MUSIC
(www.sunflowerfest.org; Aug) Tends to draw bigger names than the Juke Joint Festival, and has a significant gospel component.

🛏 Sleeping & Eating

Riverside Hotel   HISTORIC HOTEL $
(662-624-9163; ratfrankblues@yahoo.com; 615 Sunflower Ave; r with/without bath $75/65;) Don't let a well-worn exterior put you off: this hotel, soaked in blues history – blues singer Bessie Smith died here when it was a hospital, and a festival's worth of blues artists, from Sonny Boy Williamson II to Robert Nighthawk have stayed here – offers clean and tidy rooms and sincere friendliness. It's been family-run since 1944, when it was 'the black hotel' in town. The original proprietor's son, Rat, will charm your socks off with history, hospitality and prices.

Shack Up Inn   INN $
(662-624-8329; www.shackupinn.com; 001 Commissary Circle; Hwy 49; d $75-165;) At the Hopson Plantation, this self-titled 'bed and beer' allows you to stay in refurbished sharecropper cabins or the creatively renovated cotton gin. The cabins have covered porches and are filled with old furniture and musical instruments. Years of being the most storied accommodation in Clarksdale have bred complacency, however, and service can be indifferent.

Larry's Hot Tamales   AMERICAN $
(662-592-4245; 947 Sunflower Ave; mains $4-12; 11am-11pm Mon-Sat) Friendly Larry's may have a small menu, but it's doing the Lord's work with what's on offer: sizzling hot Delta tamales and delicious rib tips. You'll bust your stomach way before you bust your wallet.

Yazoo Pass   CAFE $$
(662-627-8686; www.yazoopass.com; 207 Yazoo Ave; lunch $6-10, dinner $13-26; 7am-9pm Mon-

ARKANSAS DELTA

Roughly 120 miles east of Little Rock, and just 20 miles from Clarksdale, Hwy 49 crosses the Mississippi River into the Arkansas Delta. Helena, a formerly prosperous but currently depressed mill town with a blues tradition (Sonny Boy Williamson II made his name here), awakens for its annual Arkansas Blues & Heritage Festival (www.kingbiscuitfestival.com; tickets $45; ☉ Oct) when blues musicians and their fans take over downtown for three days in early October. Year-round, blues fans and history buffs should visit the Delta Cultural Center (☑870-338-4350; www.deltaculturalcenter.com; 141 Cherry St; ☉9am-5pm Tue-Sat) FREE. The museum displays all manner of memorabilia such as Albert King's and Sister Rosetta Tharpe's guitars, and John Lee Hooker's signed handkerchief.

The world's longest-running blues radio program, *King Biscuit Time*, is broadcast here (12:15pm Monday to Friday), and *Delta Sounds* (1pm Monday to Friday) often hosts live musicians; both air on KFFA AM-1360. Before leaving town, make like Robert Plant and stop by the wonderfully cluttered Bubba's Blues Corner (☑870-338-3501; 105 Cherry St, Helena, AR; ☉9am-5pm Tue-Sat; ❢) to pick up a blues record.

The hardscrabble railroad town of McGehee is the home of the touching WWII Japanese American Internment Museum (☑870-222-9168; 100 South Railroad St; admission $5; ☉10am-5pm Tue-Sat). During World War II, Japanese Americans were rounded up and evicted from their homes and businesses and sent to live in internment camps. One of these camps took root in the delta mud just outside McGehee, and this museum is dedicated to telling the story of its inmates via personal items, art and a small collection of intimate displays.

Sat; ☎) A contemporary space where you can enjoy fresh scones and croissants in the mornings, salad bar, sandwiches and soups at lunch, and pan-seared ahi, filet mignon, burgers and pastas at dinner.

⭐ Entertainment

Red's
BLUES

(☑662-627-3166; 395 Sunflower Ave; cover $7-10; ☉live music 9pm Fri & Sat) Clarksdale's best juke joint, with its neon-red mood lighting, plastic-bag ceiling and general soulful disintegration, is the place to see bluesmen howl. Red runs the bar, knows the acts and slings a cold beer whenever you need one.

Ground Zero
BLUES

(☑662-621-9009; www.groundzerobluesclub.com; 0 Blues Alley; ☉11am-2pm Mon & Tue, to 11pm Wed & Thu, to 2am Fri & Sat) For blues in polished environs, Morgan Freeman's Ground Zero is a huge and friendly hall with a dancefloor surrounded by tables. Bands take to the stage Wednesday to Saturday, and there's good food available.

🛍 Shopping

Cat Head Delta Blues & Folk Art
ARTS & CRAFTS

(☑662-624-5992; www.cathead.biz; 252 Delta Ave; ☉10am-5pm Mon-Sat) Friendly St Louis carpetbagger and author Roger Stolle runs a colorful, all-purpose, blues emporium. The shelves are jammed with books, face jugs, local art and blues records. Stolle seems to be connected to everyone in the Delta, and knows when and where the bands will play.

Around Clarksdale

Down Hwy 49, Tutwiler is where the blues began its migration from oral tradition to popular art form. Here, WC Handy, known as the Father of the Blues, first heard a sharecropper moan his 12-bar prayer while the two waited for a train in 1903. That meeting is immortalized by a mural at the Tutwiler Tracks (off Hwy 49; ❢).

East of Greenville, Hwy 82 heads out of the Delta. The Highway 61 Blues Museum (☑662-686-7646; www.highway61blues.com; 307 N Broad St; ☉10am-5pm Mon-Sat), at the start of the route known as the 'Blues Highway,' packs a mighty wallop in a condensed, six-room space venerating local bluesmen from the Delta. Leland hosts the Highway 61 Blues Festival in late September or early October. Highway 61 itself is a legendary road that traverses endless, eerie miles of flat fields, Gothic agricultural industrial facilities, one-room churches and moldering cemeteries.

Stopping in the tiny Delta town of Indianola is worthwhile to visit the modern BB King Museum and Delta Interpretive

Center (☎ 662-887-9539; www.bbkingmuseum.
org; 400 Second St; adult/student/child $15/5/free;
⊙ 10am-5pm Tue-Sat, noon-5pm Sun-Mon, closed
Mon Nov-Mar). While the museum is dedicated
to the legendary bluesman, it also tackles life
in the Delta as a whole. This is the best museum in the region, filled with interactive displays, video exhibits and an amazing array of
artifacts, effectively communicating the history and legacy of the blues while shedding
light on the soul of the Delta.

Vicksburg

Lovely Vicksburg sits atop a high bluff overlooking the Mississippi River. For 47 days
during the Civil War, General Ulysses S Grant
attacked the city until its surrender on July 4,
1863, which meant the North gained dominance over North America's greatest river.

◎ Sights

The major sights are readily accessible from
I-20 exit 4B (Clay St). Charming historic
downtown stretches along several cobblestoned blocks of Washington St. Down by the
water is a block of murals depicting the history of the area, and a Children's Art Park.

Vicksburg National Military Park   BATTLEFIELD
(☎ 601-636-0583; www.nps.gov/vick; Clay St; per
car/individual $8/4; ⊙ 8am-5pm; 🚻) ⦿ Vicks-
burg controlled access to the Mississippi
River, and its seizure was one of the turning points of the Civil War. A 16-mile driving
tour passes historic markers explaining battle scenarios and key events from the city's
long siege, when residents lived like moles

THACKER MOUNTAIN RADIO

If you find yourself driving a lonely
Mississippi back road or concrete strip
of interstate on a Saturday evening at
7pm, turn your radio dial to the local
NPR frequency (www.mpbonline.org/
programs/radio for a listing). You'll
be treated to Thacker Mountain
Radio, a Mississippi variety show that
showcases some of the region's finest
authors and musicians. It's an enjoyable
means of getting under the cultural skin
of this state, and the music ain't half
bad either. You can see the show being
recorded at 6pm on Thursday nights at
Off Square Books in Oxford (129 Courthouse Sq) during fall and spring.

---

in caverns to avoid Union shells. Plan on
staying for at least 90 minutes. If you have
your own bike, cycling is a fantastic way to
tour the place. Locals use the scenic park for
walking and running.

Lower Mississippi River Museum   MUSEUM
(☎ 601-638-9900; www.lmrm.org; 910 Washington
St; ⊙ 9am-4pm Wed-Sat; 🚻) ⦿ FREE Downtown Vicksburg's pride and joy is this surprisingly interesting museum which delves
into such topics as the famed 1927 flood
and the Army Corps of Engineers, who have
managed the river since the 18th century.
Kids will enjoy the aquarium and clamber-
ing around the dry-docked research vessel,
the M/V Mississippi IV.

🛏 Sleeping & Eating

Corners Mansion   B&B $$
(☎ 601-636-7421; www.thecorners.com; 601 Klein
St; r $125-170; 🅿✱🖵) The best part of this
wedding-cake 1873 B&B is looking over the
Yazoo and Mississippi Rivers from your
porch swing. The gardens and Southern
breakfast don't hurt either.

Walnut Hills   SOUTHERN $$
(☎ 601-638-4910; www.walnuthillsms.net; 1214
Adams St; mains $8-25; ⊙ 11am-9pm Mon-Sat, to
2pm Sun) For a dining experience that takes
you back in time, head to this eatery where
you can enjoy rib sticking, down-home
Southern food elbow-to-elbow, family-style.

☕ Drinking & Nightlife

★ Highway 61 Coffeehouse   CAFE
(☎ 601-638-9221; www.61coffee.blogspot.com;
1101 Washington St; ⊙ 7am-5pm Mon-Fri, from 9am
Sat; 🖵) ⦿ This awesome coffee shop has occasional live music on Saturday afternoons,
serves Fair Trade coffee and is an energetic
epicenter of artsiness, poetry readings and
the like.

Jackson

Mississippi's capital and largest city mixes up stately residential areas with large
swaths of blight, peppered throughout with
a surprisingly funky arts-cum-hipster scene
in the Fondren District. There's a slew of decent bars, good restaurants and a lot of love
for live music; it's easy to have a good time
in Jackson.

Canons at Vicksburg National Military Park

◉ Sights

Smith Robertson Museum   MUSEUM
See p46.

Mississippi Museum of Art   GALLERY
(☑ 601-960-1515; www.msmuseumart.org; 380 South Lamar St; special exhibitions $5-12; ⊙10am-5pm Tue-Sat, noon-5pm Sun) **FREE** This is your must-stop sight when visiting Jackson. The collection of Mississippi art – and the permanent exhibit dubbed 'The Mississippi Story' – is superb, and the surrounding grounds are nicely landscaped into a bright and quirky garden area.

Old Capitol Museum   MUSEUM
(www.mdah.state.ms.us/museum; 100 State St; ⊙9am-5pm Tue-Sat, 1-5pm Sun) **FREE** The state's Greek Revival capitol building from 1839 to 1903, it now houses a Mississippi history museum filled with films and exhibits. You'll learn that secession was far from unanimous, and how reconstruction brought some of the harshest, pre-segregation 'Black Codes' in the South.

Eudora Welty House   HISTORIC BUILDING
(☑ 601-353-7762; www.eudorawelty.org; 1119 Pinehurst St; adult/student/child $5/3/free; ⊙tours 9am, 11am, 1pm & 3pm Tue-Fri) Literature buffs should make a reservation to tour the Pulitzer Prize–winning author's Tudor Revival house, where she lived for more than 75 years. It's now a true historical preservation down to the most minute details. It's free on

the 13th day of any month, assuming that's a normal operating day.

Museum of Natural Science   MUSEUM
(☑ 601-576-6000; www.mdwfp.com/museum; 2148 Riverside Dr; adult/child $6/4; ⊙8am-5pm Mon-Fri, from 9am Sat, from 1pm Sun; 🚹) 🌿 Tucked way back in Lefleur's Bluff State Park is the Museum of Natural Science. It houses exhibits on the natural flora and fauna of Mississippi, and has aquariums inside, a replica swamp and 2.5 miles of trails traversing 300 acres of preserved prettiness.

🛏 Sleeping & Eating

The Fondren District is the budding artsy, boho area of town, with restaurants, art galleries and cafes dotting the happening commercial strip.

Old Capitol Inn   BOUTIQUE HOTEL **$$**
(☑ 601-359-9000; www.oldcapitolinn.com; 226 N State St; r/ste from $99/145; 🅿 ❄ @ 🛜 ⛴) This 24-room boutique hotel, located near museums and restaurants, is terrific. The rooftop garden includes a hot tub. A full Southern breakfast (and early-evening wine and cheese) is included, and the rooms are all comfortable and uniquely furnished.

Big Apple Inn   AMERICAN **$**
(☑ 601-354-4549; 509 N Farish St; mains $2; ⊙7:30am-9pm Tue-Fri, from 8am Sat) The Big Apple basically has two items on its menu: a hot sausage sandwich and a pig's ear

Old Capitol Museum (p117)

NAGEL PHOTOGRAPHY/SHUTTERSTOCK ©

sandwich. Both are small, served on soft rolls, and taste delicious. The interior is hot, cramped and dingy, and the surrounding neighborhood is fading fast, but this is a true Jackson original, and the pig's ear is worth a long drive.

High Noon Cafe VEGETARIAN $
(☑ 601-366-1513; www.rainbowcoop.org; 2807 Old Canton Rd; mains $7-10; ☺11:30am-2pm Mon-Fri; 🛜☑) 🍃 Tired of fried, green, pulled-pork-covered catfish? This organic vegetarian grill, inside the Rainbow Co-op grocery store in the Fondren District, does beet burgers, portabello Reubens and other healthy delights. Stock up on organic groceries too.

Saltine SEAFOOD $$
(☑ 601-982-2899; www.saltinerestaurant.com; 622 Duling Ave; mains $12-19; ☺11am-10pm Mon-Thu, to 11pm Fri & Sat, to 9pm Sun) This playful spot takes on the delicious task of bringing oysters to the Jackson culinary world. The bivalves are served in several iterations: raw, woodfired, with Alabama white barbecue sauce and 'Nashville' *(very)* hot. Sop up some shellfish sauce with the excellent skillet cornbread, then give the grilled rainbow trout a whirl.

Walker's Drive-In SOUTHERN $$$
(☑ 601-982-2633; www.walkersdrivein.com; 3016 N State St; mains lunch $10-17, dinner $26-36; ☺11am-2pm Mon-Fri & from 5:30pm Tue-Sat) This retro masterpiece has been restored with

love and infused with new Southern foodie ethos. Lunch is diner 2.0 fare with grilled redfish sandwiches, tender burgers and grilled oyster po'boys, as well as an exceptional seared, chili-crusted tuna salad, which comes with spiced calamari and seaweed.

🍷 Drinking & Entertainment

Martin's BAR
(☑ 601-354-9712; www.martinslounge.net; 214 S State St; ☺10am-1:30am Mon-Sat, to midnight Sun) This is a delightfully dirty dive, the kind of place where the bartenders know the phone numbers of their regulars in case said regulars pass out on their bar stools. Attracts a mix of old-timers, statehouse workers, slick lobbyists and lawyers plucked from a John Grisham novel. Live music and karaoke spice up weekends.

Sneaky Beans CAFE
(☑ 601-487-6349; www.sneakybeans.tumblr.com; 2914 N State St; ☺7am-9:30pm Mon-Fri, from 7:30am Sat) Every city deserves a great cafe with fast wi-fi, quirky art and an airy sense of space; Sneaky Beans, which also boasts a pretty great library, is Jackson's contribution to the genre.

The Apothecary at Brent's Drugs COCKTAIL BAR
(www.apothecaryjackson.com; 655 Duling Ave; ☺5pm-1am Tue-Thu, to 2am Fri & Sat) Tucked into the back of a '50s-style soda fountain shop is a distinctly early 21st-century craft cocktail bar, complete with bartenders sporting thick-framed glasses, customers with sleeve tattoos and a fine menu of expertly mixed libations.

F Jones Corner BLUES
(☑ 601-983-1148; www.fjonescorner.com; 303 N Farish St; ☺11am-2pm Tue-Fri, 10pm-late Thu-Sat) All shapes and sizes, colors and creeds descend on this down-home Farish St club when everywhere else closes. It hosts authentic Delta musicians who have been known to play until sunrise.

Hal & Mal's LIVE MUSIC
(☑ 601-948-0888; www.halandmals.com; 200 Commerce St) Hal & Mal's is simply an excellent midsized live-music venue. The sight lines are great, it feels neither too crowded nor annoyingly expansive, bar service is quick and whoever is doing the booking is killing it, bringing in a range of acts that speak to Jackson's under-appreciated capacity for funkiness.

❶ Information

Convention & Visitors Bureau (☏ 601-960-1891; www.visitjackson.com; 111 E Capitol St, Suite 102; ⊗ 8am-5pm Mon-Fri) Free information.

❶ Getting There & Away

At the junction of I-20 and I-55, it's easy to get in and out of Jackson. Its international **airport** (JAN; ☏ 601-939-5631; www.jmaa.com; 100 International Dr) is 10 miles east of downtown. **Greyhound** (☏ 601-353-6342; www.greyhound. com; 300 W Capitol St) buses serve Birmingham, AL, Memphis, TN, and New Orleans, LA. Amtrak's *City of New Orleans* stops at the station.

Natchez

Some 668 antebellum homes pepper the oldest civilized settlement on the Mississippi River (beating New Orleans by two years). Natchez is also the end (or the beginning!) of the scenic 444-mile Natchez Trace Pkwy, the state's cycling and recreational jewel. Just outside of town, along the Trace, you'll find Emerald Mound (☏ 800-305-7417; Mile 10.3, Natchez Trace Pkwy; ⊗ dawn-dusk; 🚶🏊), the grassy ruins of a Native American city that includes the second-largest pre-Columbian earthworks in the USA.

Tours of the historic downtown and antebellum mansions leave from the visitor and welcome center (☏ 800-647-6724; www.visitnatchez.org; 640 S Canal St; tours adult/child $12/8; ⊗ 8:30am-5pm Mon-Sat, 9am-4pm Sun; 🚶).

🛏 Sleeping & Eating

Mark Twain Guesthouse GUESTHOUSE **$**
(☏ 601-446-8023; www.underthehillsaloon.com; 33 Silver St; r without bath $65-85; 🌀 🛜) Mark Twain used to crash in room 1, above the bar at the current Under the Hill Saloon (25 Silver St; ⊗ 9am-late), when he was a riverboat pilot passing through town. There are three rooms in all. They share one bath and laundry facilities. Check-in for the guesthouse is at the saloon.

Historic Oak Hill Inn INN **$$**
(☏ 601-446-2500; www.historicoakhill.com; 409 S Rankin St; r incl breakfast from $135; 🅿 🌀 🛜) Staying at this classic Natchez B&B, you'll get a taste of antebellum aristocratic living, from period furniture to china. A charmingly high-strung staff makes for an immaculate experience.

Magnolia Grill AMERICAN **$$**
(☏ 601-446-7670; www.magnoliagrill.com; 49 Silver St; mains $13-20; ⊗ 11am-9pm Sun-Thu, to 10pm Fri & Sat; 🚶) Down by the riverside, this attractive wooden storefront grill with exposed rafters and outdoor patio is a good place for a pork tenderloin po'boy or a fried crawfish spinach salad.

Cotton Alley CAFE **$$**
(☏ 601-442-7452; www.cottonalleycafe.com; 208 Main St; mains $10-20; ⊗ 11am-2pm & 5:30-9pm Mon-Sat) This cute whitewashed dining room is chocablock with knickknacks and artistic touches, and the menu borrows from local tastes. Think: grilled chicken sandwich on Texas toast or jambalaya pasta, but it does a nice chicken Caesar and a tasty grilled salmon salad, too.

Driving in the USA

With a comprehensive network of interstate highways, an enthusiastic car culture and jaw-dropping scenery, the USA is an ideal road-tripping destination.

Driving Fast Facts

→ **Right or left?** Drive on the right.

→ **Legal driving age** 16

→ **Top speed limit** 65mph (70mph on some Virginia highways)

→ **Best Bumper Sticker** What if the Hokey Pokey IS What It's All About?

DRIVER'S LICENSE & DOCUMENTS

All drivers must carry a driver's license, the car registration and proof of insurance. If your license is not in English, you will need an official translation or an International Driving Permit (IDP). You will also need a credit card in order to rent a car.

INSURANCE

Liability All drivers are required to obtain a minimum amount of liability insurance, which would cover the damage that you might cause to other people and property in case of an accident. Liability insurance can be purchased from rental-car companies for about $12 per day.

Collision For damage to the rental vehicle, a collision damage waiver (CDW) is available from the rental company for about $18 a day.

Alternative sources Your personal auto insurance may extend to rental cars, so it's worth investigating before purchasing liability or collision from the rental company. Additionally, some credit cards offer reimbursement coverage for collision damages if you rent the car with that credit card; again, check before departing. Most credit-card coverage isn't valid for rentals of more than 15 days or for exotic models, SUVs, vans and 4WD vehicles.

RENTING A CAR

Rental cars are readily available at regional airports and in major towns. Rates usually include unlimited mileage. Dropping the car off at a different location from where you picked it up generally incurs a substantially higher fee. Of course, shop around on price-comparison websites. Renting a car without a major credit card is difficult, if not impossible. Most agencies rent child safety seats but you should reserve in advance.

Every major car-rental company operates in the area including:

Alamo (www.goalamo.com)

Avis (www.avis.com)

Budget (www.budget.com)

Dollar (www.dollar.com)

BORDER CROSSING

Crossing the US–Canada border at Niagara Falls, the St Lawrence Seaway (Wellesley Island State Park, Ogdensburg or Massena) or on Hwy 87 north of Champlain, NY, on the way to Montreal is generally straightforward, though lines can be a hassle. All travelers entering the USA are required to carry passports, including citizens of Canada and the USA. If you're driving a rental car from Canada or Mexico you'll need documentation from your rental-car company showing permission to bring the car to another country (check the policy before making the trip). Otherwise, you'll simply need documentation proving you're the owner of the vehicle.

MAPS

Detailed state-highway maps are distributed free by state governments. You can call or write to state tourism offices to request maps, or they can be picked up at tourism offices.

Another excellent map resource is **DeLorme Mapping Company** (www. delorme.com), which publishes individual state maps – atlas-style books with detailed coverage of backcountry roads. The scales range from 1:65,000 to 1:135,000. The Mid-Atlantic box set includes Delaware, Maryland, New York, Pennsylvania, Virginia and West Virginia for $75.

ROADS & CONDITIONS

The quality of roadways varies widely, from potholed, suspension-killing sections of 'expressways' to smooth-as-glass highways, to sandy, rocky and everything-in-between rural byways. Rush-hour traffic around major cities could test the patience of Buddha. In the DC area, each lasts as long as three to four hours, and tunnels and bridges into and out of NYC can be backed up for miles. Northern Virginia is a nightmare of exits and fast interchanges between major roads.

➡ Road signage is not always well-placed or easy to interpret.

➡ One-way streets can make navigation in some cities and towns difficult.

➡ Roads to the region's beaches and shore areas are best avoided on Friday afternoons and Sunday evenings. Tune into local radio stations for traffic updates, especially at these times.

Tolls

The shortest and fastest route between two points often means taking a toll road. Most bridge and tunnels call for a toll though usually not in both directions. Consider paying for an E-Z Pass account in advance to speed things up, avoid having to scrounge around for bills and change,

Driving Problem Buster

What should I do if my car breaks down? Call the service number of your car-hire company and a local garage will be contacted. If you're driving your own car, it's a good idea to join AAA, who can be called out to breakdowns at any time. Many car insurance companies also offer roadside assistance.

What if I have an accident? If there are no serious injuries and your car is operational, move over to the side of the road. If there are serious injuries, call 911 for an ambulance. Exchange information with the other driver, including names, contact and insurance info, and license tag numbers. Then file an accident report with the police or Department of Motor Vehicles.

What should I do if I get stopped by the police? Stay in your car and keep your hands visible. The police will want to see your driver's license and proof of liability insurance. As long as you're not a serious threat, you probably won't end up in the pokey, although you'll probably get either a ticket or a warning if you've broken a road rule.

Will my E-Z Pass work in every state in the region? Yes, E-Z Pass, the electronic toll collecting system used in the northeastern US, is integrated so that you can pay tolls everywhere regardless of the state agency you are registered with.

Road Trip Websites

American Automobile Association
(AAA; www.aaa.com) Provides
maps and other information, as well
as travel discounts and emergency
assistance for members.

Cost of Tolls (www.costoftolls.
com) Latest prices for all bridges,
tunnels and roadways in the area.

Gas Buddy (www.gasbuddy.com)
Find the cheapest places to gas
up nearby.

Traffic.com (www.traffic.com) Real-
time traffic reports, with details
about accidents and traffic jams.

and for reduced rates. Otherwise, tolls can
be hefty. The following is only a short list:

➡ Atlantic City Expwy (connects Philly and AC)

➡ Gov Thomas E Dewey Thruway, New York
(I-90)

➡ New Jersey Turnpike and John F Kennedy
Memorial Hwy (I-95)

➡ Pennsylvania Turnpike (I-76)

➡ Delaware Rte 1 (103-mile long highway from
Maryland border to I-95)

➡ Dulles Toll Rd (Rte 267) Northern Virginia

➡ Chesapeake Bay Bridge Tunnel (Virginia's
Eastern Shore to Virginia Beach)

ROAD RULES

The maximum speed limit on most
freeways is 65mph; Virginia has some
sections where it is 70mph. Police in
cruisers and unmarked cars enforce
speed limits with varying degrees of
intensity.

Other road rules:

➡ Driving laws are different in each state, but
most require the use of safety belts. Texting
while driving is prohibited.

➡ Unless otherwise indicated, making a right
turn on a red light is allowed.

➡ Children under four years of age must be
placed in a child safety seat secured by a
seat belt.

➡ Most states require motorcycle riders to
wear helmets whenever they ride. In any case,
the use of a helmet is highly recommended.

PARKING

In the countryside parking is generally free.
In cities you will have to pay at a parking
meter (the cheapest), in a designated lot
or structure, or you can look for free neighborhood street parking. There is usually
a time limit, and occasionally permit-only
parking, so read the signs, or you may get
an expensive ticket.

FUEL

Gas stations are extremely common,
except in national parks and high in the
mountains, though you will never be more
than 50 miles (at the very most) from
a gas station. The vast majority sell unleaded, unleaded plus and premium gas,
as well as diesel. Unleaded is cheapest and
will be fine for your rental car.

The majority gas stations are self-
service. Most pumps have credit-/debit-
card terminals built into them, so you can
pay with plastic without interacting with
a cashier. Fuel prices change frequently
and vary according to location; on average,
expect to pay $3.50 to $3.90 per gallon.

Loyalists swear by their favorite service
stations which include gas and conveni-
ence stores: two behemoths in the area
are Wawa, in eastern Pennsylvania, Virginia and Maryland, and Sheetz, found in
Maryland, West Virginia, Virginia, North
Carolina and Pennsylvania.

SAFETY

Traffic around urban areas is thick. Construction is virtually nonstop so sudden
changes in traffic patterns and obstacles
can arise without too much warning.

In urban areas especially, travelers are
advised to always remove valuables and
lock all car doors. Cities such as Memphis
certainly have their rougher areas, though
driving through any neighborhood in day-
light is rarely a problem.

Country roads usually lack road lights,
and unless you are used to dark highways
it can be intimidating. Generally, these are

also the highways where cows or deer may try to cross the road. Be very careful. Cows kill. Seriously.

- - - - - - - - - - - - - - - - - - -

RADIO

DC WAMU (88.5FM) for NPR; WKYS (93.9FM) Good for hip-hop and R & B.

Georgia 107.9 FM, Atlanta's premier hip-hop station deluxe.

Maryland WTMD (87.9FM) Great college station in Baltimore; WRNR (103.1FM) does good rock out of Annapolis.

Mississippi WABG (960 AM) Broadcasting blues from the Mississippi Delta.

New Jersey WFMU (91.1FM) DJs have free rein to indulge their idiosyncratic interests.

Pennsylvania WXPN (88.5FM) Public radio station broadcasting from UPenn.

Tennesee WEVL (89.9 FM) Memphis' only listener-supported, independent radio station, broadcasting blues, rock, world, and bluegrass music. WRLT (100.1 FM), Lightening 100, Nashville's independent radio station brings

a number of local and well-known artists into the studio.

Virginia WBRF (98.1FM) Does classic country and bluegrass in southwestern Virginia.

- - - - - - - - - - - - - - - - - - -

MID-ATLANTIC PLAYLIST

➡ **Take Me Home Country Roads**
John Denver

➡ **My Blue Ridge Mountain Boy**
Dolly Parton

➡ **Gonna Fly Now (Theme from Rocky)**
Nelson Pigford & DeEtta Little

➡ **In the Jailhouse Now** Jimmie Rodgers

➡ **East Virginia Blues**
Ralph Stanley & The Clinch Mountain Boys

➡ **Turkey in the Straw** Dock Boggs

➡ **Mule Skinner Blues** Dolly Parton

➡ **Hey, Good Lookin'** Tennessee Ernie Ford

➡ **Keep on the Sunny Side** Carter Family

➡ **My Clinch Mountain Home**
Carter Family

➡ **Blue Eyes Crying in the Rain**
Willie Nelson

BEHIND THE SCENES

SEND US YOUR FEEDBACK

We love to hear from travelers – your comments help make our books better. We read every word, and we guarantee that your feedback goes straight to the authors. Visit **lonelyplanet.com/contact** to submit your updates and suggestions.

Note: We may edit, reproduce and incorporate your comments in Lonely Planet products such as guidebooks, websites and digital products, so let us know if you don't want your comments reproduced or your name acknowledged. For a copy of our privacy policy visit lonelyplanet.com/privacy.

ACKNOWLEDGMENTS

Climate map data adapted from Peel MC, Finlayson BL & McMahon TA (2007) 'Updated World Map of the Köppen-Geiger Climate Classification', *Hydrology and Earth System Sciences*, 11, pp1633–44.

Illustration pp60-1 by Javier Martinez Zarracina.

Cover photographs: Old Stone House Manassas Battlefield, Zoonar GmbH/Alamy; Back: Bloody Lane, Antietam National Battlefield, Michael Melford/Getty Images

THIS BOOK

This 1st edition of *Civil War Trail Road Trips* was researched and written by Amy C Balfour, Michael Grosberg, Adam Karlin, Kevin Raub, Adam Skolnick, Regis St Louis and Karla Zimmerman. This guidebook was produced by the following:

Destination Editor Dora Whitaker

Product Editors Catherine Naghten, Kathryn Rowan

Senior Cartographer Alison Lyall

Book Designers Virginia Moreno, Wendy Wright

Assisting Editors Imogen Bannister

Assisting Cartographers Mick Garrett, Julie Sheridan, Diana von Holdt

Cover Researcher Naomi Parker

Thanks to Shahara Ahmed, Sasha Baskett, Kate Chapman, Brendan Dempsey, James Hardy, Indra Kilfoyle, Katherine Marsh, Darren O'Connell, Katie O'Connell, Kirsten Rawlings, Angela Tinson, Tony Wheeler

OUR STORY

A beat-up old car, a few dollars in the pocket and a sense of adventure. In 1972 that's all Tony and Maureen Wheeler needed for the trip of a lifetime – across Europe and Asia overland to Australia. It took several months, and at the end – broke but inspired – they sat at their kitchen table writing and stapling together their first travel guide, *Across Asia on the Cheap*. Within a week they'd sold 1500 copies. Lonely Planet was born.

Today, Lonely Planet has offices in Melbourne, London and Oakland, with more than 600 staff and writers. We share Tony's belief that 'a great guidebook should do three things: inform, educate and amuse'.

INDEX

000 Map pages

000 Map pages

OUR WRITERS

Amy C Balfour A Southerner, she's been visiting the Outer Banks since she was a child and never tires of running down Jockey's Ridge. Amy has authored or co-authored more than 15 books for Lonely Planet, including *Hawaii* and *Southwest USA*.

Michael Grosberg Thanks to an uncle and aunt's house upstate on the Delaware River in the southern Catskills, Michael has had a base from which to explore the region for two decades – that is, when he's not home in Brooklyn, NYC. No matter his love for the city, getaways are necessary and he's taken every opportunity to travel far and wide.

Adam Karlin Born in Washington, DC and raised in rural Maryland, Adam has written close to 40 guidebooks for Lonely Planet, covering areas from the Andaman Islands to the Zimbabwe border, but the place he decided to settle is New Orleans, one of his favorite cities in the world.

Kevin Raub Kevin Raub started his career as a music journalist in New York, but he it for travel writing and moved to Brazil. Living outside the country, it's fair to say he immensely enjoyed gorging on Nashville hot chicken, Memphis BBQ, craft beer out the wazoo and various other unmentionables on his voyage through the Southern US. Follow him on Twitter (@RaubOnTheRoad).

Adam Skolnick Adam writes about travel, culture, health and politics for Lonely Planet, *Outside*, *Men's Health* and *Travel & Leisure*. He has co-authored 20 Lonely Planet guidebooks and blames the state of Kentucky for his growing bourbon dependency. You can read more of his work at www.adamskolnick.com, or find him on Twitter and Instagram (@adamskolnick).

Regis St Louis Regis grew up in a sleepy riverside town where he dreamed of big-city intrigue. He's lived all over the US, and has crossed the country by train, bus and car while visiting remote corners of America. Favorite memories from his most recent trip include crab feasting on Maryland's eastern shore and catching music jams in the Blue Ridge Mountains of Virginia.

Karla Zimmerman As a life-long Midwesterner, Karla is well versed in the region's beaches, ballparks, breweries and pie shops. When she's not home in Chicago watching the Cubs, and writing, she's out exploring. For this gig, she covered DC, where she never fails to shake hands with Racing Abe Lincoln at Nationals Park. Karla has written for several Lonely Planet guides to the USA, Canada, Caribbean and Europe.

Published by Lonely Planet Publications Pty Ltd
ABN 36 005 607 983
1st edition – May 2016
ISBN 978 1 76034 047 6
© Lonely Planet 2016   Photographs © as indicated 2016
10 9 8 7 6 5 4 3 2 1
Printed in China